How
Desktop
Publishing
Works

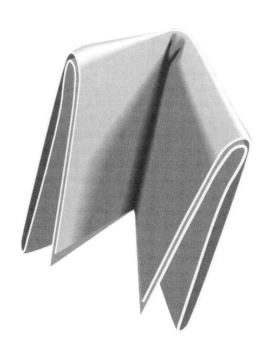

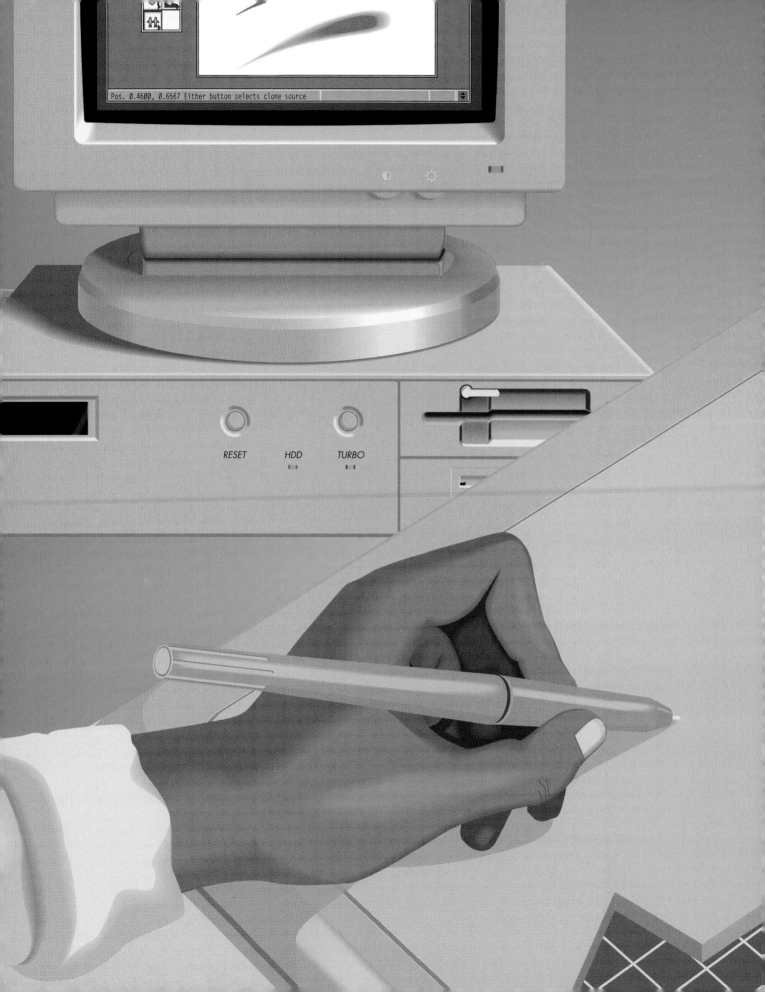

Pos. 0.4600, 0.6567 Either button selects clone source

RESET   HDD   TURBO

HOW DESKTOP PUBLISHING WORKS

PAMELA PFIFFNER
BRUCE FRASER

Illustrated by
DAVE FEASEY

Ziff-Davis Press
Emeryville, California

Senior Development Editor	Melinda E. Levine
Copy Editor	Kelly Green
Technical Reviewer	John Taschek
Project Coordinator	Barbara Dahl
Proofreader	Carol Burbo
Cover Illustrator	Dave Feasey
Cover Designer	Carrie English
Series Book Designer	Carrie English
Illustrator	Dave Feasey
Contributing Illustrators	Pamela Drury Wattenmaker, K. Daniel Clark, Timothy Edward Downs, and Michael Troller
Word Processor	Howard Blechman
Layout Artist	Bruce Lundquist
Digital Prepress Specialist	Joe Schneider
Indexer	Ted Laux

Ziff-Davis Press books are produced on a Macintosh computer system with the following applications: FrameMaker®, Microsoft® Word, QuarkXPress®, Adobe Illustrator®, Adobe Photoshop®, Adobe Streamline™, MacLink®*Plus*, Aldus® FreeHand™, Collage Plus™.

If you have comments or questions or would like to receive a free catalog, call or write:
Ziff-Davis Press
5903 Christie Avenue
Emeryville, CA 94608
1-800-688-0448

ISBN 1-56276-191-9

Manufactured in the United States of America

10 9 8 7 6 5 4 3 2 1

**To our parents:
Pat and Dave Pfiffner, and
Jan and Cam Fraser**

Introduction xi

PART 1

Introduction to Desktop Publishing
1

Chapter 1
A Brief History
of Publishing...........................4

Chapter 2
What Is Desktop
Publishing? 10

Chapter 3
What You Need to Desktop
Publish...................................18

PART 2

Page Layout and Type
24

Chapter 4
What Is Page Layout?...........28

Chapter 5
What Is Type? 34

Chapter 6
How Digital Fonts Work 42

Chapter 7
How a Page Layout Program
Works 50

PART 3

Graphics
56

Chapter 8
Traditional Graphics 62

Chapter 9
Computer Graphics...............68

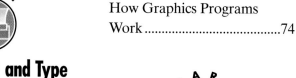

Chapter 10
How Graphics Programs
Work 74

PART 4

Color
82

Chapter 11
What Is Color?.......................86

Chapter 12
Printed Color..........................94

Chapter 13
Computer Color 100

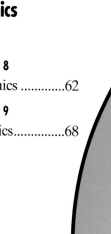

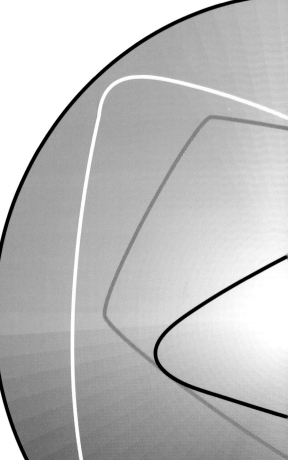

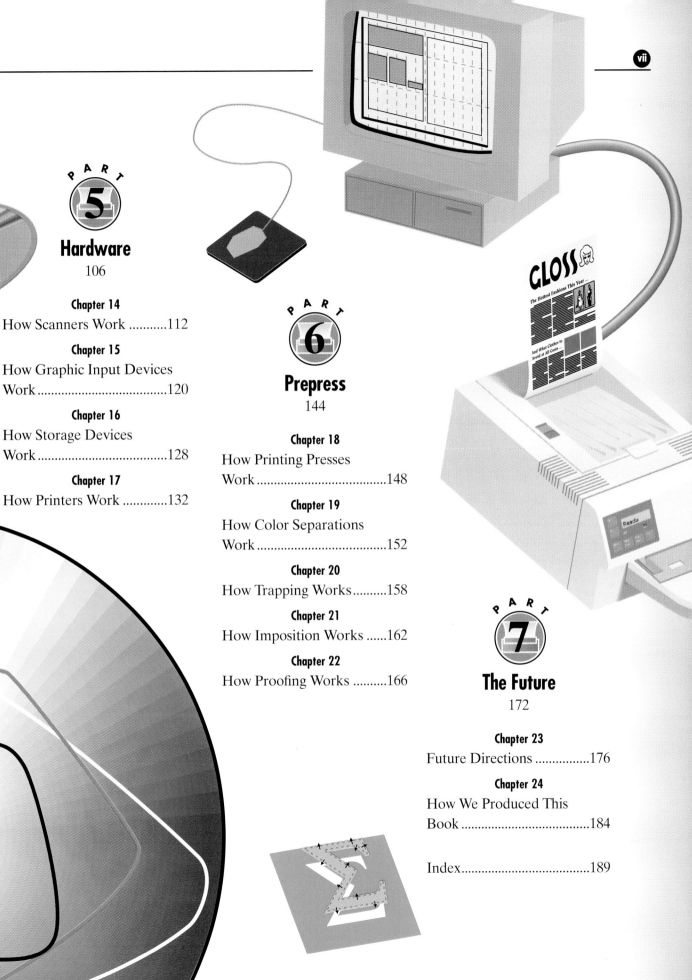

PART 5
Hardware
106

Chapter 14
How Scanners Work 112

Chapter 15
How Graphic Input Devices
Work 120

Chapter 16
How Storage Devices
Work 128

Chapter 17
How Printers Work 132

PART 6
Prepress
144

Chapter 18
How Printing Presses
Work 148

Chapter 19
How Color Separations
Work 152

Chapter 20
How Trapping Works 158

Chapter 21
How Imposition Works 162

Chapter 22
How Proofing Works 166

PART 7
The Future
172

Chapter 23
Future Directions 176

Chapter 24
How We Produced This
Book 184

Index....................................189

We'd like to thank our friends and colleagues at *MacUser* and *MacWEEK* magazines for the opportunity to work and share ideas with them. Thanks, too, to our friends in the typographic, printing, and imaging communities for their generosity in sharing their knowledge and time with us over the years. And to our pals (you know who you are) who questioned the wisdom of our working together: We did it anyway.

Pamela Pfiffner
Bruce Fraser
San Francisco

We're often asked, "What is desktop publishing?" Some will say that desktop publishing is simply a tool, and in a narrow sense they're right. But new tools can lead both to fundamental change in the work for which they're used and to entirely new kinds of work. Marshall McLuhan pointed out the far-reaching effects of such a simple tool as the electric light, which turned night into day and changed our patterns of sleep, of commerce, and of travel.

But like any new invention, the electric light had its costs. Our frenetic open-24-hours lifestyle is more stressful than one whose rhythms are dictated by the gentle dance of sun and moon. City-dwellers spend their lives never seeing the constellations of the night sky, let alone learning their names and their places in the turning of the seasons. We may lament these costs, but we accept the benefits unquestioningly—few of us wish to return to the dark ages.

Desktop publishing may not have had as profound an impact as the electric light, but it has wrought irrevocable change on print publishing, and many have been all too ready to lament the costs. It's true that desktop publishing has spawned plenty of pages that would make a trained designer wince, but it has also democratized publishing as no other invention before it, and it has undoubtedly improved the quality and readability of everyday printed communication.

Desktop publishing has scrambled job descriptions and even wiped out some traditional occupations, but it has also streamlined the publishing process and made it more cost-effective. As a result, we have a greater diversity of print than ever before.

When we first started exploring desktop publishing in 1985, we sensed a revolution was in the air. Taking to heart Stewart Brand's aphorism that "when it comes to technology, you're either part of the steamroller or part of the road," we cast our lot with the steamroller. Through equal parts of luck and judgment, we were fortunate enough to participate in the birth of that revolution.

We had no formal training when we started desktop publishing in 1985. Using the first Macintosh model available and the first commercial Macintosh desktop publishing software, we made clumsy newsletters and résumés. As the hardware and software improved, we began producing more polished publications. Before we knew it, desktop publishing was a full-time occupation, eventually leading us to work for national magazines that are produced via desktop publishing. We've never looked back.

That progression from the individual working alone with a single computer to many people and machines collaborating on a publication mirrors the development of desktop publishing systems. Personal computers are integrated into publishing systems that produce the major newspapers and magazines that you read daily, weekly, and monthly, as well as the book you hold now in your hands.

In this book we've tried to give you an overview of the concepts, tools, and processes that constitute desktop publishing. It isn't a how-to book. We won't tell you how to become—or be a better—desktop publisher. But we will show you how it all comes together, from page layout to print-ing press. Whether you're a novice just thinking about putting together that first newsletter, a graphic artist exploring the basics of color printing, or a traditionalist considering buying that first computer system, we hope you'll find something of value in this book.

The terminology of desktop publishing has its roots in ancient forms of communication. The goal of desktop publishing is the same as that of any other method: to create a printed piece that conveys the message to the reader effectively and persuasively. We believe that understanding the history of publishing only enhances your experience of desktop publishing, so we've given this book a foundation by showing how publishing has evolved from metal type to today's digital tools.

If you're interested in learning more about the rich history of publishing and typography, we recommend *Printing Types, Volumes 1 and 2* by Daniel Berkeley Updike, *The Thames and Hudson Manual of Typography* by Ruari McLean, and *Printing Presses* by James Moran. An indispensable guide to the entire publishing process, both contemporary and traditional, is *Pocket Pal* by the International Paper Corporation.

There are many fine books that teach how to design publications or how to use specific programs or both. Buy them, read them, use them. But since the essence of desktop publishing is the power it gives individuals to create their own publications, we encourage you to jump in, play around, and experiment. (Remember to save your work often.) You'll discover your own sense of style, and you'll learn more to boot.

Writing *How Desktop Publishing Works* has given us the opportunity to distill many years of experience into an easy-to-read primer, but there is so much more involved, so much more that we could have said, and so much more to come as desktop publishing continues to evolve. We hope this book will get you hooked on desktop publishing so you, too, can participate in enriching our written heritage.

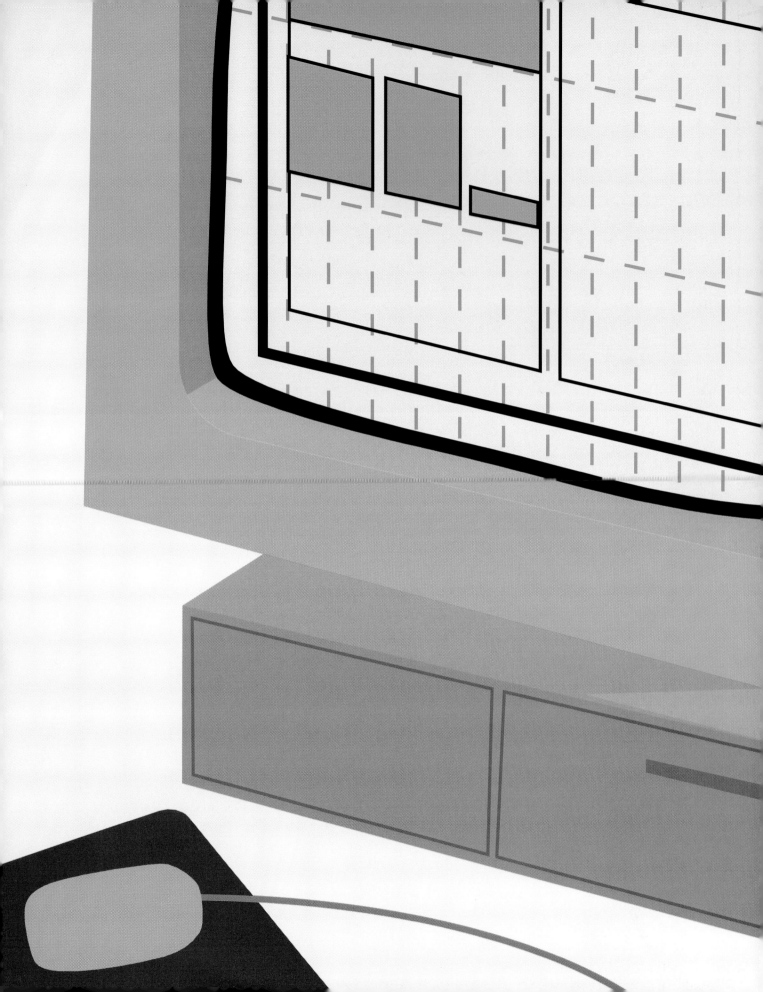

INTRODUCTION TO DESKTOP PUBLISHING

CONTENTS

Chapter 1: A Brief History of Publishing
4

Chapter 2: What Is Desktop Publishing?
10

Chapter 3: What You Need to Desktop Publish
18

DESKTOP PUBLISHING IS just the latest milestone in publishing's rich history. The urge to communicate is endemic to humankind, as attested to by cave-wall paintings recording successful hunting parties. But the urge to publish involves not only creating these recordings of daily life, but reproducing them and distributing them to others.

The history of publishing is intimately linked to the development of printing, paper, ink, type, and in later years, of the photographic process. These elements combine to produce words and images on paper that can be mass-produced and freely distributed. We may live to see paper replaced by CD-ROMs or TV screens, and ink replaced by coded patterns of magnetism, electricity, or light, but the basis of publishing—the broad dissemination of words and images—has remained essentially unchanged for thousands of years.

Despite the lure of brave new technologies, printed matter is still the preferred way of distributing ideas—whether writing a letter to your lawyer, faxing your elected representative, reading the latest scandal sheet, losing yourself in the pages of a novel, or surrendering to the tactile appeal of a finely printed coffee-table book. This flexibility remains unmatched by any other medium, and accounts for the widespread popularity and use of the printed page.

At the dawn of the personal computer era, the pundits predicted that the widespread adoption of computers would give rise to the paperless office. Instead, the amount of printed matter produced by businesses has exploded. At the same time, the quality of the appearance of everyday business communication has improved. The business community has learned that good design communicates the message more effectively— a well-designed document stands out and demands attention, a commodity in increasingly short supply.

Despite the dramatic impact the personal computer has had on the world of publishing, the fundamental elements of printed communication have changed surprisingly little. Text and images are still integrated into a layout and pages are produced, but desktop publishing has changed the way we approach these tasks. The phrase *desktop publishing* was coined by Aldus Corporation founder Paul Brainerd, an ex-newspaperman turned computer entrepreneur, as a name for the new process of using personal computers to integrate computer-generated type and graphics into electronic pages, which are in turn printed on digital printing devices such as laser printers and imagesetters.

In its early years, desktop publishing was synonymous with poor-quality documents, partly through limitations of the technology and partly through inexperience on the part of the practitioners. But now desktop publishing has so permeated the entire field of publishing, from club newsletters to metropolitan dailies, from small-press self-help books to finely printed art reproductions, that some find the term meaningless and argue for its abolition, preferring simply to call it publishing.

With the adoption of the new technology, the clear division of labor among editors, artists, designers, and production workers has become blurred. Some traditional publishing occupations, such as typesetting, have almost ceased to exist; others, such as color stripping and dot-etching, are fast disappearing as both the workflow and the production processes themselves change to accomodate or exploit technological innovation.

To help you understand how desktop publishing works, and where it fits in the grand scheme of things, let's review how publishing has been done in the past, and how it's done using the new tools; then we'll take a look at what you need in order to do desktop publishing yourself.

A Brief History of Publishing

N O ONE CAN pinpoint the exact date when humans first started communicating by means of marks made on a surface. We know that some form of writing existed in the sixth century B.C., but these symbols or ideographs represented specific people, places, and things. The development of the phonetic alphabet can be traced to about 2000 B.C. when the Phoenicians, a seafaring culture residing on the eastern shores of the Mediterranean, used writing primarily to record their trading activities.

Until the invention of the printing press, publishing meant writing by hand—initially on clay tablets, eventually on vellum made from skins of such animals as calf or sheep. Paper was invented by the Chinese in A.D. 100, but it took about a thousand years for the techniques of making paper out of plant fiber to reach Europe. In fact, printing in Asia predates that in Europe by a good 700 years. The Chinese, Japanese, and Koreans devised printing methods using carved wooden blocks. But these languages used alphabets containing more than 40,000 characters rather than the 26 or so used in European languages, so the economic impact of movable type was less profound than it would be in Europe some 700 years later.

Before printing came to Europe, books were produced in scriptoria; trained writers sat in a room transcribing words read to them or hand-copying books laid before them. Writing was a specialized and secretive art often confined to monasteries. Many believe that the most beautiful books ever made are the illuminated manuscripts produced in Ireland in the Middle Ages, around A.D. 700. But hand production made books both rare and costly.

The invention of modern publishing is generally credited to Johannes Gutenberg, a goldsmith in Mainz, Germany. Gutenberg and his imitators were able to produce books at a theretofore unthinkable rate, and the explosion of knowledge that his invention made possible was in large part responsible for the Renaissance. In the 1440s, Gutenberg began experimenting with a printing system that used *movable type*, individual pieces of lead with raised letters that could be assembled into words and lines of type, then disassembled and reused after printing. Although the development of movable type saddled Gutenberg with insurmountable debts, it made the business of publishing, as we know it, possible. Books were no longer unique hand-produced items, and literacy was no longer confined to the church and monastery.

As Gutenberg's invention swept across Europe, distinctive styles of type developed, influenced by the handwriting style of the region as well as by the skill of the printer in cutting and casting the type in lead. Gutenberg duplicated the black letter style of handwriting popular in Northern Europe at the time. As printing moved south into Italy and France, roman and italic styles emerged. Typefaces developed in the sixteenth, seventeenth, and eighteenth centuries by Claude Garamond, William Caslon, Giambattista Bodoni, and John Baskerville form the backbone of today's typography.

Assembling individual pieces of type into words and lines—compositing, or *typesetting*, as it later became known—was a time-consuming process requiring highly skilled labor. Setting type involved picking individual letters out of type drawers or cases (the genesis of the terms *uppercase* and *lowercase*) and placing them in a metal vice (a composing stick) upside down so that they would read properly when printed.

Gutenberg's system of printing continued essentially unchanged for some 400 years, until the Industrial Revolution. Metal gradually replaced the wooden parts, making stronger presses that could run faster; rotary presses replaced the slower flatbed presses; and hand power was replaced by horse, by waterwheel, and eventually, by steam. A further development in the early 1800s was continous-roll paper—called the *web*. By the mid-1850s, the newspaper age was firmly under way, driven by rotary-web-fed presses capable of printing newspapers at the rate of 10,000 impressions per hour.

In the late 1880s, a new invention relieved printers of the time-consuming process of setting type by hand: the line-casting machine. In a process that became known as *hot type*, the machine dropped the matrices, or molds, in place, then poured hot metal into the mold, creating a single piece of metal containing the entire line (called the *slug*). Now a typesetter could sit at a keyboard and type in whole lines. Machines made by Monotype and Linotype set the standard, each offering type that worked exclusively with their respective equipment.

The new art of photography had its impact on the publishing process, too. Photo-engraving began to replace the time-consuming process of hand-engraving plates for image reproduction. The halftone process, which represents a photograph's gray tones with tiny, variable-sized black dots, made it possible to reproduce photographs in newsprint. In the 1920s, halftoning was combined with the work done on color photography dyes, and the four-color print process was born. The entire range of color can be represented using only four inks—cyan, magenta, yellow, and black—printed as superimposed halftones. Process color printing, as it became known, is the method used for most full-color printing up to the present day.

In the 1950s, photographic processes came to type. In phototypesetting, characters stored on transparent film were projected onto photosensitive paper. Different sizes of the same type could be obtained by changing lenses. Fast and economical, phototypesetting—dubbed *cold type*—quickly replaced hot type, completing the switch from mechanical to optical processes in page composition.

In the late 1970s, the first digital typesetters appeared: floppy disks replaced the fragile photographic fonts. At the same time, some pioneers began to use electronic scanners rather than cameras to capture images for reproduction. These early ventures into the digital domain were a direct precursor to desktop publishing, as we'll see in the next chapter.

A Brief History of Publishing

Ancient Approaches

The development of the phonetic alphabet by the Phoenicians in the second millenium B.C. shaped the history of the written word in western civilization. Unlike alphabets based on ideograms, which contained 40,000 or more characters, the phonetic alphabet represented language using only 26 or so symbols.

Illuminated Manuscript

The books produced by the Celtic church in Ireland in the eighth century represented the peak of the scribe's art. But such books were unique, costly, and difficult to read.

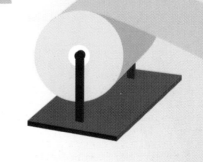

Printing Press c. 1450

Gutenberg adapted a wine press to make a printing press. His 42-line Bible, published in 1455, is considered to have heralded the birth of modern publishing. About 180 Bibles were printed (30 copies are believed to have been printed on vellum, requiring 170 calves per Bible). Gutenberg's type drawers contained 300 characters, letter combinations, and punctuation marks. Today's printers use about 50.

Rotary-Web Press c. 1865

By the 1850s, rotary presses made of metal had largely replaced the old wooden flatbed presses. The development of the "endless sheet" of paper, the web, made it possible for steam- or water-powered rotary-web presses to feed the growing demand for mass-circulation newspapers.

Halftone

The halftone process works by exploiting an optical illusion. If different-sized, regularly spaced dots are printed in a sufficiently fine grid pattern, the eye sees them as shades of gray rather than as clusters of dots. The halftone process made it possible to re-produce photographs in print, first in black and white, and later in color.

Linotype Machine c. 1890

The Linotype machine allowed the typesetter to compose type using a keyboard: It automatically positioned the *matrices* (or molds) for entire lines of type, then cast each line in a *slug* (a single piece of lead).

Phototypesetting

In phototypesetting machines, each character was stored as a transparent shape on a piece of opaque film. The characters in a font were arranged on a wheel or a strip. When the typesetter pressed a key on the keyboard, the appropriate character would rotate into position in front of a light source and an arrangement of lenses, which projected the character's shape onto photosensitive paper. Using lenses of different focal lengths, different sizes of type could be produced from the same character outline.

Digital Type

In digital type, the character's shapes are recorded as mathematical descriptions. Digital typesetting machines use a grid of tiny dots (typically 1,200 to 2,500 per inch) that are so finely spaced that they appear continuous to the naked eye. When a character is called for in a particular size, the computer in the digital typesetter calculates which dots to print and which to leave blank to produce the type on the photosensitive paper.

What Is Desktop Publishing?

ORE THAN 500 years after Gutenberg created movable type, another development had an equally revolutionary impact on publishing: the personal computer. Although computers had been used to drive photographic typesetting machines, they were not publishing machines unto themselves until 1985.

To understand the changes wrought by desktop publishing, let's look at the traditional publishing process. Whether it's done by one person or one hundred, the publishing process integrates content (words and graphics) and form (design and production). Writers and editors produce words, and artists create graphics. Designers create layouts into which text and graphics must fit. Typesetters turn edited text into strips of copy (galleys) according to the designer's specifications. The galleys, along with any graphics, are turned over to paste-up artists who assemble the elements into pages. The pasted-up pages are photographed and the film positives or negatives are taken to the printing plant where they're turned into plates ready for the printing press.

Now imagine if you could do all these steps on your personal computer. That's desktop publishing.

Desktop publishing was unleashed upon the world in 1985, thanks to three key events: Apple Computer introduced its LaserWriter printer; Adobe Systems included its PostScript page-description language in the LaserWriter; and Aldus Corporation revealed its PageMaker software. The synergy between these developments gave rise to what Aldus founder Paul Brainerd dubbed "desktop publishing."

Before Apple introduced the Macintosh in 1984, computer printers were essentially typewriters that produced only text. That same year, Apple produced the ImageWriter I, a dot-matrix printer that printed graphics as well as text, but its low resolution made for coarse text and pictures. The LaserWriter's higher resolution offered near-typeset quality, and Adobe's page-description language meant that type and graphics could be scaled in size. PostScript also contributed another key factor: device independence, which guaranteed that files printed on one PostScript printer would print identically on other PostScript printers.

Aldus PageMaker put the software equivalent of a layout table into the hands of the personal computer owner. Text could be imported from a word processing program and set in columns according to specifications set within PageMaker. Type could be any size or style. Graphics could be inserted with a few keystrokes. Then, at the push of button, an entire page could be printed out on an Apple LaserWriter with all graphics and type styles and sizes intact.

Now anyone equipped with a Macintosh, LaserWriter, and PageMaker could be a publisher. Journalist A.J. Liebling's old saw "The power of the press belongs to those who own one" was never more appropriate. And just as the invention of movable type eliminated the need for scribes, so the advent of high-resolution film-based PostScript output devices—called imagesetters—decimated the ranks of typesetters, and gave birth to the service-bureau industry.

With the widespread introduction of PostScript imagesetters by established traditional companies like Linotype and Monotype, desktop publishing turned professional. Thanks to the magic of PostScript, you can proof pages on a laser printer, then take them to a service bureau for high-quality output on film, knowing that your final pages would look like your proofs, only better.

As desktop publishing pioneers, we can attest to the glitches of that early era, but nearly ten years later, desktop publishing has evolved into a successful industry. Sophisticated software allows you to edit photographic images or draw complex illustrations. New printing technologies let you print color graphics quickly without leaving your office. Ever-faster and more powerful personal computers make it easier than ever to produce professional-looking publications. No wonder magazines as diverse as *The New Yorker* and *Playboy* use desktop publishing tools for the bulk of their production tasks.

But despite increased sophistication, desktop publishing can still be done by the individual, as we'll see in the next chapter when we discuss the equipment you need.

The Traditional Publishing Process

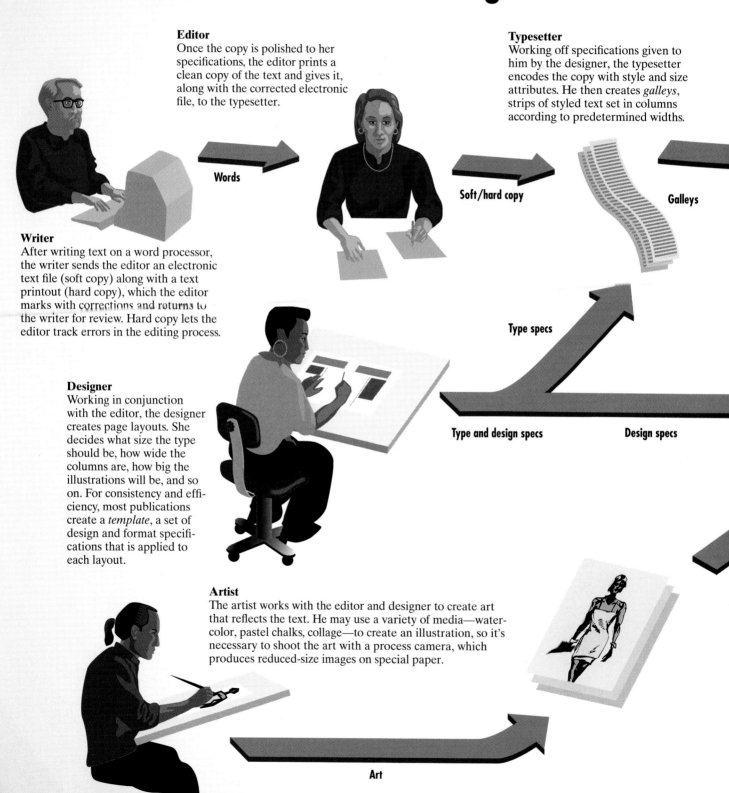

Editor
Once the copy is polished to her specifications, the editor prints a clean copy of the text and gives it, along with the corrected electronic file, to the typesetter.

Typesetter
Working off specifications given to him by the designer, the typesetter encodes the copy with style and size attributes. He then creates *galleys*, strips of styled text set in columns according to predetermined widths.

Words

Soft/hard copy

Galleys

Writer
After writing text on a word processor, the writer sends the editor an electronic text file (soft copy) along with a text printout (hard copy), which the editor marks with corrections and returns to the writer for review. Hard copy lets the editor track errors in the editing process.

Type specs

Designer
Working in conjunction with the editor, the designer creates page layouts. She decides what size the type should be, how wide the columns are, how big the illustrations will be, and so on. For consistency and efficiency, most publications create a *template*, a set of design and format specifications that is applied to each layout.

Type and design specs

Design specs

Artist
The artist works with the editor and designer to create art that reflects the text. He may use a variety of media—watercolor, pastel chalks, collage—to create an illustration, so it's necessary to shoot the art with a process camera, which produces reduced-size images on special paper.

Art

Camera Operator
The boards are sent to the camera operator. They're photographed with a special camera to create film negatives of the entire page.

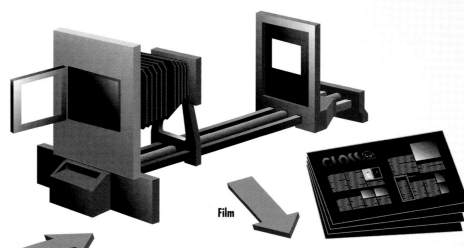

Film

Boards

Paste-up Artist
The type galleries and camera-ready art are handed over to the paste-up department for integration into the designer's layout. Here the type and art are cut, trimmed, and pasted (using a special wax) onto stiff boards.

Camera-ready art

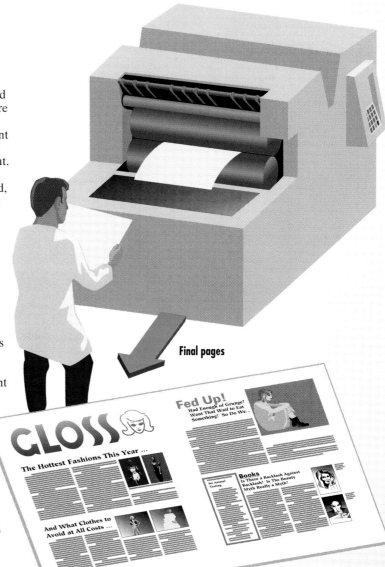

Final pages

Press Operator
In order to proof the film, the press operator first exposes the negatives onto either photosensitive paper (in the case of black and white) or onto a laminated substrate (in the case of color). The proof shows what the final print job will look like.

Next, the proofed film negatives are exposed onto special photosensitive material, which will be used as printing plates on the press. (On critical jobs, a press proof, printed on the actual printing press, is made as a final check prior to the press run.)

Then, the final pages are printed on the press. Depending on the nature of the press and of the job, pages may be printed one at a time, or grouped together on a sheet that can be folded and cut to produce a group of pages (a *signature*). *Perfecting* presses print both sides of the paper in a single pass. The pages are trimmed and bound into books or folded into newspapers.

The Desktop Publishing Process

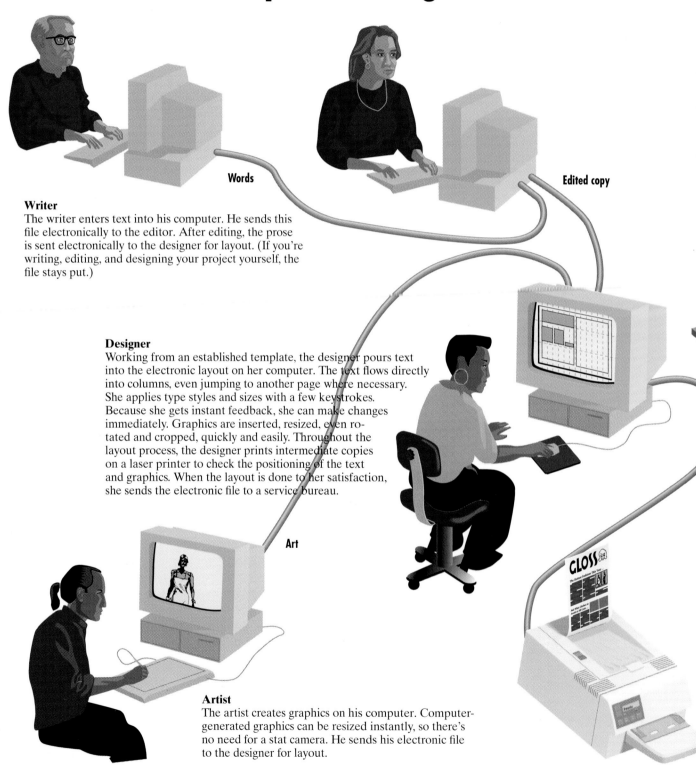

Words

Edited copy

Writer
The writer enters text into his computer. He sends this file electronically to the editor. After editing, the prose is sent electronically to the designer for layout. (If you're writing, editing, and designing your project yourself, the file stays put.)

Designer
Working from an established template, the designer pours text into the electronic layout on her computer. The text flows directly into columns, even jumping to another page where necessary. She applies type styles and sizes with a few keystrokes. Because she gets instant feedback, she can make changes immediately. Graphics are inserted, resized, even rotated and cropped, quickly and easily. Throughout the layout process, the designer prints intermediate copies on a laser printer to check the positioning of the text and graphics. When the layout is done to her satisfaction, she sends the electronic file to a service bureau.

Art

Artist
The artist creates graphics on his computer. Computer-generated graphics can be resized instantly, so there's no need for a stat camera. He sends his electronic file to the designer for layout.

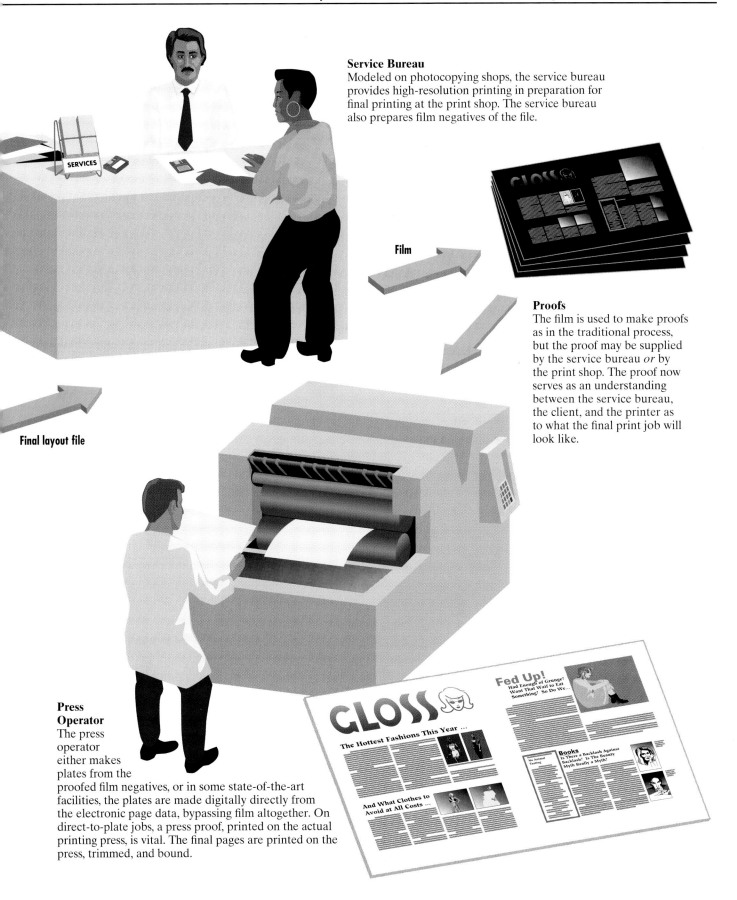

Service Bureau
Modeled on photocopying shops, the service bureau provides high-resolution printing in preparation for final printing at the print shop. The service bureau also prepares film negatives of the file.

Film

SERVICES

Proofs
The film is used to make proofs as in the traditional process, but the proof may be supplied by the service bureau *or* by the print shop. The proof now serves as an understanding between the service bureau, the client, and the printer as to what the final print job will look like.

Final layout file

Press Operator
The press operator either makes plates from the proofed film negatives, or in some state-of-the-art facilities, the plates are made digitally directly from the electronic page data, bypassing film altogether. On direct-to-plate jobs, a press proof, printed on the actual printing press, is vital. The final pages are printed on the press, trimmed, and bound.

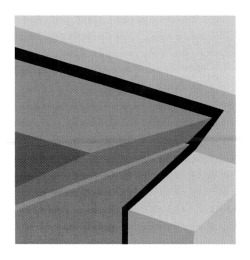

What You Need to Desktop Publish

THE DESKTOP PUBLISHING process is the same for all publishers, whether you're one person with a computer or fifty people on a multinode network. What began as a scaled-down version of the traditional publishing process has now come full circle: a large-scale collaborative effort. Desktop publishing, initially the domain of the lone individual, has been scaled up to meet the needs of the most demanding professionals.

Whether the publishing project is a small-circulation newsletter or a glossy magazine, the tools are essentially the same. All desktop publishing systems contain the same building blocks: the computer, input and output devices, and publishing software.

Since we've designed this book to be as platform-neutral as possible, we won't argue the merits of one system over another. The tools are fundamentally the same on all computer platforms, but desktop publishing begs for a WYSIWYG (what-you-see-is-what-you-get) operating system, such as that found on the Apple Macintosh or on IBM-compatible computers running Microsoft Windows. Desktop publishing originated on the Macintosh, so the tools are more evolved on that platform, and it has been more readily adopted in professional publishing. But Apple's dominance in desktop publishing is being challenged by the overwhelming success of Windows.

Input devices are mechanisms for getting content into your computer. A mouse is an input device, as is the keyboard with which you type words into your computer. A scanner lets you bring images into your computer. *Scanners* are similar to photocopying machines—a light source shines on the image, producing light that is captured by a detector—but scanners translate that light into digital data rather than sending it back out as hard copy.

Output devices let you get information back from your computer. The monitor screen is an output device, as are printing units that produce hard copy. These range from desktop ink-jet and laser printers in black and white or color, to high-resolution imagesetters that print on photosensitive paper or film.

To put it all together you need software. In some situations a page layout program may be all you need: Most let you do word processing and graphic design within the application. But page layout programs import a wide variety of formats, so you'll probably want the extra functionality of stand-alone word processors, illustration packages, image editors, and other graphics software. You'll also need digital typefaces (commonly called *fonts*, which, as we'll explain later, is actually a misnomer).

Which hardware and software you choose depends largely on the scale of the project. For example, scanners are indispensable tools for transforming photographs and line art into digital data, but the kind of scanner needed varies according to the demands of your publication: Will it require black-and-white or color images? Are your originals photographic prints or transparencies? Will your final pages be photocopied or printed on a high-quality press? What is your budget? The answers to these questions will help you decide which tools are appropriate for your desktop publishing system.

In the following pages, we outline the basic components of a desktop publishing system. We'll look at these tools in detail later. To help you choose the tools that best suit your needs, we've identified three representative types of publications: a small-scale black-and-white newsletter, journal, or book, usually published by one person (we'll call this level 1); a medium-size newsletter, magazine, or book, that uses color highlights but the publisher turns to a service bureau for high-resolution output and to a print shop to strip in photographs and other elements (we'll call this level 2); and a larger newspaper or magazine, or an image-heavy book, which has all its color images and page layouts produced in-house (we'll call this level 3).

What You Need to Desktop Publish

Applications
Neat software abounds in desktop publishing, but four types of programs are vital: a page layout program; a word processing program; fonts or typefaces, either in PostScript or TrueType format; and a graphics program either for drawing line art or for creating painted-type images. If you plan to work with photographic images, you'll also need an image editing program.

Monitor
Your monitor is the window through which you view all your efforts. If you're working exclusively in black and white, you can use a black-and-white monitor. If you plan to use photographic images, a gray-scale monitor is preferable. If your work includes color, you'll obviously need a color monitor. In any case, high resolution is essential.

Desktop printer
A black-and-white PostScript-compatible laser printer is critical to any desktop publishing operation. If your final output is to be photo-copied or if you plan to use a service bureau, a laser printer may be all you need. Even if you plan to work in color, desktop laser printers let you print sample layouts and type tests more quickly and cheaply than is possible with color printers. Ink-jet printers are much slower than lasers without a cor-responding savings in price.

Computer
Your computer is the nerve center of your desktop publishing operation. Since desktop publishing makes heavy demands on the machine, you'll want the fastest processor (central processing unit or CPU) and the most memory (random access memory or RAM) you can afford.

Storage device
When it comes to storage devices, bigger is always better. Layouts, graphics, fonts, and the applications themselves all combine to hog hard-disk space. For simple projects, a 100-megabyte hard disk is a modest choice. You also need some means of backing up your valuable data. Small projects can fit on a floppy disk, but for larger projects, removable media such as a Syquest drive and car-tridges or magnetic optical drives and disks are useful. Most service bureaus are also equipped to accept jobs on removable cartridges.

Scanner
Scanners convert either flat art, such as photographic prints and line art, or photographic transparencies into computer data for incorporation into your publication. Three types of scanners are used for publishing: flatbed, slide, and drum. Flatbeds are the least expensive; the drum scanners used in professional prepress shops can cost more than $100,000.

LEVEL 1

LEVEL 2

LEVEL 3

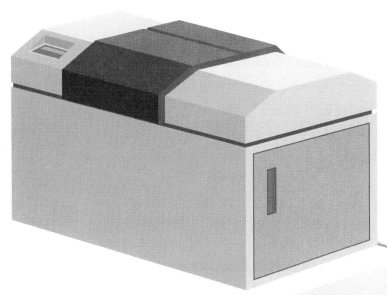

Imagesetter
Imagesetters aren't for everyone—they're generally found in service bureaus and in sophisticated in-house publishing departments. These high-resolution devices produce photographic paper or film that printers use to create the plates that go on the printing press.

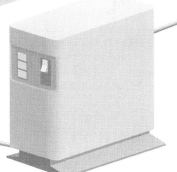

RIP (raster image processor)

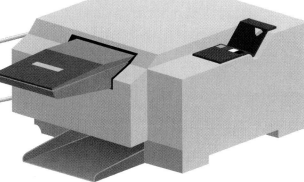

Prepress software
Publishing professionals use software designed specifically to prepare pages for the printing press, such as imposition and trapping programs.

Color printer
Low-cost color ink-jet and thermal-wax printers are a valuable adjunct to a laser printer if you plan to work in color. They're useful for creating comps—short for *comprehensives*—which show assembled pages with all color elements in place. More expensive dye-sublimination printers produce images with photorealistic quality.

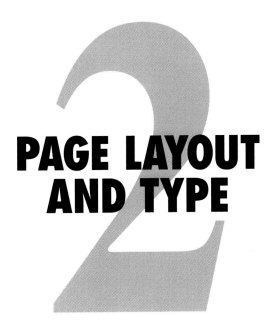

PAGE LAYOUT AND TYPE

CONTENTS

Chapter 4: What Is Page Layout?
28

Chapter 5: What Is Type?
34

Chapter 6: How Digital Fonts Work
42

Chapter 7: How a Page Layout Program Works
50

DESKTOP PUBLISHING CAN be a single-person enterprise of computer, printer, and paper, or a large-scale operation of workstations, servers, and imagesetters. But both the humblest newsletter and the glossiest magazine are based on two indispensible ingredients: page layout software and digital typefaces. Page design is the skeleton of the publication and type is its lifeblood. Therefore, the layout and typographic decisions you make are perhaps the most critical in the desktop publishing process.

There are two separate aspects of page layout: design and paste-up. Traditionally, the art director designs the pages, working within constraints imposed by editorial intent, available materials, cost effectiveness, and so on. She sketches her ideas on *dummies*, paper mock-ups of her design. The paste-up artist translates these dummies into precise layouts and incorporates text and graphics into the layout by literally pasting strips of paper onto cardboard.

In desktop publishing, the same person often designs the publication and places text and images into the electronic layout. As both artistic designer and production artist this person has to make decisions about the format and style of the publication from the beginning. One of the more attractive features of desktop publishing is the relative ease with which changes can be made, both to content and to design, right up until the last minute.

Some decisions regarding the layout are based upon practical considerations—paper size, for example. Other judgments are purely aesthetic, such as whether or not to place a box around text. In Chapter 4, we look at the anatomy of a page, and introduce the basic elements that make up the underlying structure of a page.

A readable, well-balanced publication is a blend of the practical and the aesthetic. In this latter category falls the choice of typefaces. Mastering typography is a lifelong discipline; until recently, typography was a craft practiced by an exclusive community, following rules known only to a few. Desktop publishing changed that, and in the early days at least, it wasn't necessarily a change for the better.

Anyone who buys a computer has access to dozens of typefaces, and the early days of desktop publishing were riddled with documents that resembled ransom notes with half-a-dozen mismatched typefaces littering the page. That's changing thanks to increased education about and awareness of type and typography. The number of typefaces available is growing, too. Keep in mind that purveyors of digital type are drawing on more than 500 years of type design. As a result, there are thousands (and still counting) of digital typefaces from which to choose.

But choosing a typeface is, at best, only half the battle. Knowing how to set it is also a key to attractive pages. Understanding the vocabulary of type—so much of it dates back to the days of metal type—and the goals to strive for in setting type may not turn you into a master typographer overnight, but it will open up new ways of thinking about type, and help you to produce more polished publications. In Chapter 5 we introduce type terminology, the kinds of controls used to work with type, and the situations for which the controls were designed.

When type was set by hand, each foundry had its own unique designs, which were jealously guarded. When the Linotype machine and its competitors came along, type foundries produced type that was specific to the machine on which it was used. Type remained proprietary to particular typesetting systems through the period of photographic typesetting, but with the advent of digital type, and particularly of the PostScript page-description language, typefaces suddenly became open and nonproprietary, giving designers an unprecedented freedom of choice.

However, digital typefaces come in several different computer formats, and most of those formats exist in several forms, each specific to a given computer platform; for example, PostScript and TrueType, the two most common digital-type formats, come in varieties for the Apple Macintosh or the Windows environment. Each format has its champions. In Chapter 6 we'll explain the similarities and differences and explore basics of working with type on the computer.

Page layout programs are where it all comes together. Raw text becomes polished type and is assembled together with graphics into finished pages. As the workhorses of desktop publishing, page layout programs share some common features that help you automate much of the production of a publication. In Chapter 7, we introduce some of these features, and discuss how to use them effectively and productively.

This book won't show you how to become a designer or turn you into a master typographer. There are plenty of other books that aim to do that. But by introducing the vocabulary used in design and typography, this book will provide you with a conceptual framework that you can build on through practice and further study.

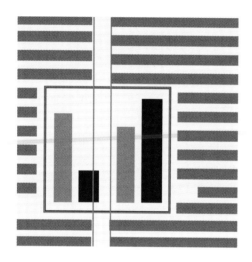

What Is a Page Layout?

THE PAGE LAYOUT is the vessel which contains your text and graphics. In fact, when describing how they put text into an electronic layout, most desktop publishers say they pour copy into the layout, and copy flows from page to page.

Some aspects of the design are global in scope—that is, once set up, they will apply to the entire document—and others may change from page to page. No matter which page layout program you use, the basic approach remains the same. Establishing the page size or format of your publication is the first step.

From the start, consider your budget. Some designs cost much more to produce and print than do others. That doesn't mean good design costs a lot to produce and bad design doesn't. But some initial choices will have a far-reaching effect on your budget. The biggest expense will likely be the final offset printing or photocopying, so you should start your planning by considering the final product.

Will your publication be photocopied or printed on a printing press? If the publication will be photocopied, it's expensive and inconvenient to use anything other than standard letter, legal, or ledger-sized paper. You can, of course, print more than one page on each sheet of paper and fold the sheet; for example, two 8-by-5½-inch pages fit on one 8½-by-11-inch sheet. If the publication will be printed on a printing press, ask your printer what paper sizes are available to you—presses come in many sizes, and some paper sizes are more economical than others. The page layout program will let you specify custom page dimensions.

Once the page size has been determined, the next step is to plan the *layout*—the arrangement of the structural elements that make up the document's page geometry. Most layouts are based on a *grid*—that is, a system of nonprinting vertical and horizontal lines that determine where elements go on a page. A grid may be as simple as one or two units, or as complex as 12 units or more. In general, the more units in the grid, the more flexible the layout—a 12-unit grid can serve as the basis for two-, three-, or four-column layouts. Once the grid is established, the next decisions, normally, are the number and width of the columns of text, and the amount of space between them. These elements form the skeleton of the publication, the bones that define its overall shape.

It's also important to learn the system of measurement used in publishing and the graphic arts: the *pica*, and its subunit, the *point*. Until computers made their impact on publishing, a point was defined as some infinitesimally small amount less than $\frac{1}{72}$ of an inch, but in desktop publishing, and in the print business generally, a point is now defined as exactly $\frac{1}{72}$ of an inch. There are 12 points in a pica and 6 picas to the inch. Type is always specified in points; page elements are measured in points and picas.

You'll encounter this measurement system when you choose typefaces for body copy, headlines and subheads, bylines, sidebars, and other elements shown in the following illustration. We'll look at type in the next chapter, but to get you started, let's look at the anatomy of a page.

What Is a Page Layout?

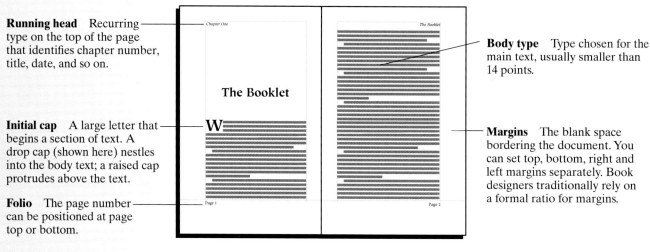

Running head   Recurring type on the top of the page that identifies chapter number, title, date, and so on.

Initial cap   A large letter that begins a section of text. A drop cap (shown here) nestles into the body text; a raised cap protrudes above the text.

Folio   The page number can be positioned at page top or bottom.

Body type   Type chosen for the main text, usually smaller than 14 points.

Margins   The blank space bordering the document. You can set top, bottom, right and left margins separately. Book designers traditionally rely on a formal ratio for margins.

Format   5½ by 8½ inches (Letter folded)

Spread   Two facing pages in a publication. It's always best to design with spreads in mind.

Banner or nameplate   The banner, or nameplate, is a standing element or logo that identifies the publication.

Deck   The deck—several lines of type—runs under the main headline and provides additional information.

Subhead   Subheads help the reader by breaking up long sections of body text and by summarizing key points to follow. Set subheads slightly larger than body text.

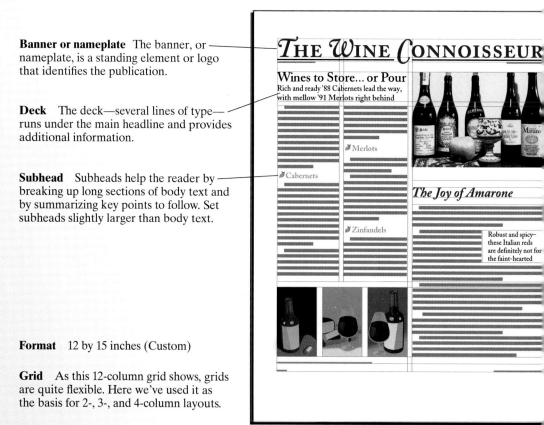

Format   12 by 15 inches (Custom)

Grid   As this 12-column grid shows, grids are quite flexible. Here we've used it as the basis for 2-, 3-, and 4-column layouts.

Display type Large typefaces with striking characteristics work well as nameplates or headlines.

Headline type The title of an article should be set in type larger than 14 points.

Pull quote Provocative text taken from a story, pull quotes help draw the reader into the story as well as break up long expanses of text.

Rule The decorative line that distinguishes sections is always measured in points.

Grid Nonprinting lines that establish an underlying structure or skeleton for the publication. This is a 3-column grid.

Box Boxes that frame text help distinguish articles, such as the supplemental text found in sidebars.

Caption Descriptive text that runs under art, the caption type should be small and distinct from body type.

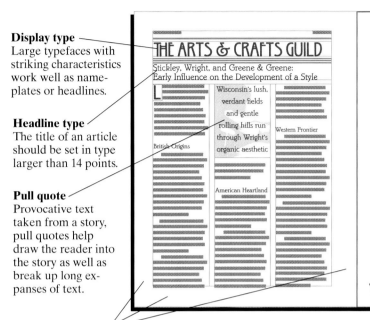

THE ARTS & CRAFTS GUILD

Stickley, Wright, and Greene & Greene: Early Influence on the Development of a Style

Wisconsin's lush, verdant fields and gentle rolling hills run through Wright's organic aesthetic

British Origins

Western Frontier

American Heartland

GUSTAV STICKLEY REMEMBERED

The Evolution of the Prairie Settle

Margins If you're designing spreads, your inside margins should be a bit wider since you'll lose some space in the binding process. If you set very narrow margins, remember that your laser printer has a limited printing area that may chop off the words.

Format 8½ by 11 inches (Letter)

Gutter The blank inner margin of a page, from the end of the printed area to the binding. The vertical space between columns is sometimes called a gutter, or an alley.

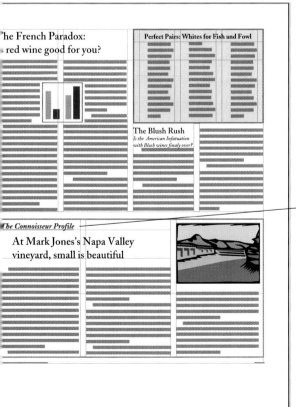

The French Paradox: Is red wine good for you?

Perfect Pairs: Whites for Fish and Fowl

The Blush Rush
Is the American Infatuation with Blush wines finaly over?

The Connoisseur Profile

At Mark Jones's Napa Valley vineyard, small is beautiful

Eyebrow An eyebrow is a short line of type that establishes a section.

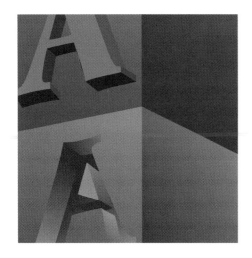

What Is Type?

METAL TYPE IS now largely confined to specialty letterpress printing, but for 500 years, metal type reigned supreme, and much of the terminology used to talk about type dates from those days. The measurement system used throughout the graphic arts—picas and points—was adopted because the point was a sufficiently small unit to describe the tiny pieces of metal used in handsetting metal type. Likewise, the term *leading*—the space between the lines—refers to the strips of lead that were once inserted between lines of metal type. Digital type is easier to set than metal, but the goals in setting type—legibility, invisibility, beauty—remain the same as they always were.

Type is meant to be read. Good typography is invisible to all but the trained eye. Bad typography, on the other hand, draws attention to itself. The range of controls that apply to type may seem bewildering, but they all help you achieve a single goal: type that can be clearly read. People don't read one word at a time; rather, they scan lines of text, reading three or four words at a glance. Body text should make it as easy as possible for the eye to move smoothly through the text. The typographic controls offered by page layout programs are all designed to solve specific problems that would otherwise interrupt this smooth movement of the eye through the text.

Choose typefaces that suit your message. Typefaces can be staid or flamboyant, formal or flashy. A typeface that works for a major company's annual report might be too cold or formal for a brochure advertising a summer camp.

For headlines and display type—short pieces of text set in sizes of 14 points and larger—suiting your typeface to your message is virtually the only requirement. But setting body text is more demanding: some characteristics that may be appealing in headline type become tiring for the reader when used extensively. Medium-weight faces tend to be more legible than very light or very heavy ones. Light faces have insufficient contrast with the background, so they are not always easily legible. In heavy faces, the distinctive differences between the letterforms are less pronounced, making the letters more difficult to read.

Conventional wisdom states that *serif* faces (typefaces with distinctive tails on vertical and horizontal lines) are more legible at text sizes, 14 points or less, than are *sans serif* faces (typefaces without serifs). Faces with extreme contrast between thick and thin strokes don't work well for body text—they create a sparkling effect that's pleasing in small quantities but quickly tires the eye.

Type set in all caps is much less legible than type set in upper- and lowercase. When type is set in all caps, all the letters have a similar size and shape, making it much harder for the eye to distinguish the letterforms.

After choosing the typeface, the type size and the leading amount should be determined. Type size will largely be dictated by column width; ideally, each line of text should be between 9 and 12 words, or about 55 to 65 characters. To achieve this, body type is usually set in sizes between 9 and 12 points, depending on the typeface.

Next, you should set the parameters for hyphenation and justification, or H&J. Body type is usually set *flush left/ragged right* (where the lines of type all line up at the left, but form a ragged right-hand margin like the type you're reading now), or *justified* (where each line is exactly the same length, creating straight margins at both ends). That's because it's very hard to read large amounts of center-aligned text with ragged right and left margins, or flush right/ragged left (which means ragged on the left with a straight right margin).

Setting type flush left is relatively straightforward: You set the desired word spacing, and the desired *hyphenation zone*—the area at the end of the text lines where the program looks for places to hyphenate words.

Justified type is more difficult to set since the program has to adjust the spacing between words and letters to make every line exactly the same length. In justified type, you set a minimum, a desired, and a maximum value for both *word spacing* (the space between words) and *letter spacing* (the space between individual characters).

About Typefaces

X-height
The size of the main body of a typeface's lowercase letters, based on the size of the letter *x*.

Ascender and ascender line
The vertical stroke that extends above the main body of such letters as *b*, *h*, and *f*.

Capital and cap line
The height of uppercase or capital letters, which is not always the same height as the ascender.

Baseline
The line on which the main body of the letter rests.

Anatomy

Descender and descender line
The vertical stroke or tail that hangs below the baseline of such letters as *g*, *j*, and *p*.

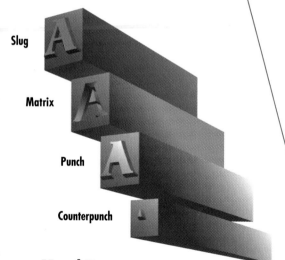

Slug

Matrix

Punch

Counterpunch

Metal Type

Punch, matrix, and metal type

Metal may be forsaken for computer pixels, but the legacy of metal type persists in today's digital type. To make metal type, the printer carved the raised letter shape on the end of a steel bar called a *punch*. If the letter contained interior spaces (an *O*, for example) he would tap a counterpunch into the punch. He then drove the punch into a copper bar to form the *matrix*, which served as a mold for the hot lead. The matrices could be reused; new sets of matrices had to be made for different sizes, however. A holdover from metal type, the *shoulder* is the small non-printing area below the letter's metal face. You can't see it in a digital typeface, but it's included in the body size of the type. That's why simply measuring a letter won't give you its accurate point size.

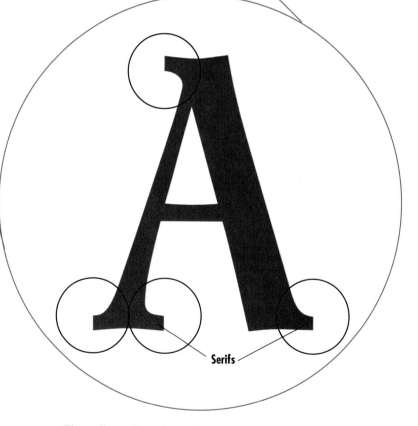

Serifs

Tiny tails on the main strokes of the letter, serifs evolved from such early lettering techniques and tools as the finishing strokes of carvers' chisels in stone and scribes' pen nibs on paper.

Counter
The space inside the enclosed area (called the *bowl*) of such letters as *a*, *o*, and *p*. When type was cast in metal, the counter was created by the counterpunch.

# of a Typeface

Type Styles

Serif
Text is often set in a serif typeface, since the horizontal lines of the serifs help lead the eye from left to right. Serif typefaces are grouped into three classes:

Old style: Dating to the 1500s, old style faces such as Garamond have little contrast between thick and thin lines.

Transitional: The first transitional typeface appeared in 1758. These typefaces, such as Bookman, have some contrast between thick and thin strokes.

Modern: Dating to the 1770s, the so-called modern typefaces such as Bodoni are identified by extreme contrast between thick and thin strokes.

Slab serif
Slab serif, or Egyptian typefaces became popular in the early nineteenth century, when they were used for architectural and advertising purposes. Their heavy lines and thick, boxy serifs make them suitable for headline and display type.

Sans serif
Sans serif typefaces—that is, typefaces without serifs—date back to ancient Greece and were rediscovered in the nineteenth century for display purposes. Now they're widely used for body text as well.

Display
Display typefaces can be serif, sans or slab serif, humorous, or in any shape you can imagine. A product of the Industrial Revolution's need to widely disseminate information via advertising, signs, and printed literature, these highly decorated faces should be used sparingly for impact.

SERIF

Garamond Old Style

Bookman Transitional

Bodoni Modern

Memphis Slab Serif

SANS SERIF

Futura

DISPLAY

ADOBE MYTHOS

The Path to Better Type

> John, by the grace of God, king of England, lord of Ireland, duke of Normandy and Aquitaine, and count of Anjou, to the archbishops, bishops, abbots, earls, barons, justiciars, foresters, sheriffs, stewards, servants, and to all his bailiffs and faithful subjects, greeting. Know that we, out of

> John, by the grace of God, king of England, lord of Ireland, duke of Normandy and Aquitaine, and count of Anjou, to the archbishops, bishops, abbots, earls, barons, justiciars, foresters, sheriffs, stewards, servants, and to all his bailiffs and faithful subjects, greeting. Know that we, out of

Leading
The space between lines of text. Too little or too much leading makes it difficult for the eye to move from line to line. Extra leading makes short lines more readable. Most page layout programs offer a default leading 2 points larger than the type size.

> John, by the grace of God, king of England, lord of Ireland, duke of Normandy and Aquitaine, and count of Anjou, to the archbishops, bishops, abbots, earls, barons, justiciars, foresters, sheriffs, stewards, servants,

Word spacing
Space between words. Too much spacing between words creates distracting gaps or rivers in the text. When setting text flush left, the word spacing should normally be set at 100 percent.

> John, by the grace of God, king of England, lord of Ireland, duke of Normandy and Aquitaine, and count of Anjou, to the archbishops, bishops, abbots, earls, barons, justiciars, foresters, sheriffs, stewards, servants, and to all his bailiffs and

Letter spacing
Space between letters. Varying the space between letters should be done only in justified text, and then only sparingly. Too much variation in the letter spacing creates dark spots where the type is clumped together.

> John, by the grace of God, king of England, lord of Ireland, duke of Normandy and Aquitaine, and count of Anjou, to the archbishops, bishops, abbots, earls, barons, justiciars, foresters, sheriffs, stewards, servants, and to all his bailiffs and faithful subjects,

> John, by the grace of God, king of England, lord of Ireland, duke of Normandy and Aquitaine, and count of Anjou, to the archbishops, bishops, abbots, earls, barons, justiciars, foresters,

John, by the grace of God, king of England, lord of Ireland, duke of Normandy and Aquitaine, and count of Anjou, to the archbishops, bishops, abbots, earls, barons, justiciars, foresters, sheriffs, stewards, servants, and to all his bailiffs and faithful subjects, greeting. Know that we, out of reverence for

John, by the grace of God, king of England, lord of Ireland, duke of Normandy and Aquitaine, and count of Anjou, to the archbishops, bishops, abbots, earls, barons, justiciars, foresters, sheriffs, stewards, servants, and to all his bailiffs and faithful subjects, greeting. Know that we, out of reverence for

Hyphenation

Breaking words at the end of lines with hyphens. If the limits you set for word and letter spacing are too inflexible, you'll end up with too many lines ending in hyphens. The key to setting justified text is to achieve a workable compromise between spacing and hyphenation.

Tracking
Tracking
Tracking
Tracking
Tracking

No Tracking
No Tracking
No Tracking
No Tracking
No Tracking

Tracking

Adding an amount of space between letters that's proportional to the point size of the type. To maintain optical regularity, type set in large sizes needs to be set somewhat tighter than the same type set in small sizes. Tracking allows you to automate this.

Kerning

Adjusting the fit of two adjacent characters. Some letter pairs don't fit well together: *To* and *Ye* are obvious examples. To maintain an even appearance, these pairs are usually *kerned*—the lowercase character is moved a little closer to the uppercase one.

Ye
To

Ye
To

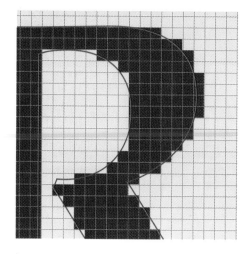

How Digital Fonts Work

WHEN TYPE WAS crafted out of lead, a printer's type collection could literally weigh a ton. Each size and style of a typeface was a new font , and a type family consisted of many fonts in different sizes and styles. Transporting a large type library from place to place was unthinkable.

Phototype, which succeeded metal type, was produced in only three sizes: small for captions, medium for text, and large for displays. Intermediate sizes were obtained by varying the focal length of the projection lens, but many shops used just one size to produce all other sizes of type. Phototype was fragile, and like metal type, would wear out with constant use.

Today's digital type is easily stored on floppy disks, tucked in shirt pockets, and taken across the country. Digital technology redefined the term *font*. Now a single design is scaled to generate all sizes of type.

Most current digital fonts use one of two core technologies: PostScript, based on the page-description language that helped launch desktop publishing, and TrueType, developed jointly by Apple Computer and Microsoft Corporation as an alternative to PostScript. To understand these technologies, you need to know how monitors and printers display pictures.

Computer displays are made up of a grid of tiny squares called *pixels* (for *picture elements*). Computers display type and other images on the screen by turning pixels on or off. This display method is called a bitmap; a *bit* (short for *binary digit*) is the smallest unit of information the computer can use, representing one of two values: on or off. Output devices such as laser printers and imagesetters also create bitmaps, but at a much higher resolution.

The first digital fonts were bitmaps—they simply told the computer which bits to turn on and which to turn off. Bitmapped fonts are still often used for screen display, but they have one disadvantage. As with metal type, each point size is a separate font. Because a bitmap is a collection of dots, when you scale it, you simply get bigger dots, so curves become jagged.

Instead of describing letters as a collection of dots, PostScript and TrueType fonts describe each character as a set of mathematical outlines. A special piece of software called a *rasterizer* uses this single outline description to create many different sizes of bitmaps at the right resolution for the output device. The rasterizer may be built into a printer, as with PostScript printers, or it may be a program that runs on the computer itself. Adobe Type Manager (ATM), a program that runs on the Macintosh and in the Windows environment, rasterizes PostScript fonts both for on-screen use and for printing to non-PostScript printers. The TrueType rasterizer is built into both the Macintosh and Windows environments, and is also included in some recent PostScript printers.

PostScript fonts consist of two separate files: a bitmapped (screen) font and an outline (printer) font. One way to visualize the difference is to think of two ways of giving someone directions. The method that corresponds to outline fonts would be, "Go to the corner, take a left, go down two blocks, then turn left at the gas station." If you were limited to the bitmap approach, you'd have to say, "Take a step. Now take another step. And another…, and so on." TrueType consolidates the bitmap data and outline data into a single file. Each format has its advantages, but the formats are functionally almost identical. More typefaces are available in PostScript format, simply because it's been around longer, but since Microsoft adopted TrueType as the native font format for the Windows environment, the number of TrueType fonts available has grown dramatically.

All computer platforms use a character set based on ASCII (American Standard Code for Information Interchange), which allows 256 characters. The first 128 characters are taken up by the upper- and lowercase alphabet, numerals, and standard punctuation. These characters are defined the same way on all computer platforms. Each platform handles the remaining 128 characters differently—they're usually used for accented characters, ligatures, and special punctuation—so translation between platforms can be problematic when using the upper 128, or the *extended set* of characters.

But 256 characters are often not enough. Metal type drawers held special characters—ligatures, swashes, flourishes, ornaments—that added typographic richness to documents. To allow desktop publishers this same richness and variety, some type vendors have created expert sets, special fonts that supplement the core font with additional characters such as old-style numbers, fractions, small capital letters, and so on. However, to use an expert set one would have to switch between the core font and its supplements, often an inelegant solution.

The proposed Unicode standard promises to remove the limitations imposed by ASCII. *Unicode* is based on 16-bit encoding, as opposed to ASCII's 8-bit encoding, thereby allowing more than 65,000 characters—essential for non-Roman alphabets such as kanji, which contains thousands of characters.

New flavors of PostScript and TrueType fonts also attempt to overcome the limitations of today's technology while preserving the typographic richness of yore. Fonts compliant with Apple's new TrueType GX format can contain up to 65,000 *glyphs* (the symbols that represent characters). TrueType GX fonts can automatically substitute the appropriate fraction or ligature for a specific combination of characters. Adobe's Multiple Master fonts contain more than one master design—a very wide version and very narrow version, for instance—so you can generate any variation in between.

Digital Font Formats

Bitmap versus Outline Fonts

Bitmap fonts, as their name implies, are simply descriptions of which pixels must be turned on and which must be turned off to reproduce a given character. Monitors typically display somewhere between 70 and 90 pixels per inch; whereas, even low-resolution laser printers use 300 dots per inch, and high-resolution imagesetters have over 2,500 dots per inch. Outline fonts describe the character shape as a set of mathematical routines, which is much more compact.

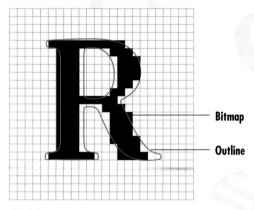

Bitmap

Outline

72 dpi

Scalability

When you scale bitmap fonts, they look ugly. Each pixel simply gets scaled up, so you quickly end up with jagged edges. Outline fonts, in contrast, can be scaled to any size.

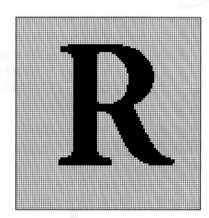

300 or higher dpi

Outline

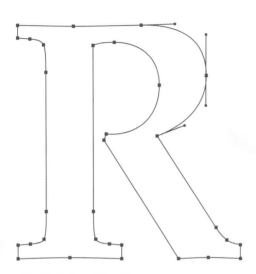

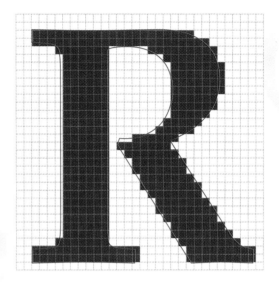

PostScript and TrueType

Both outline font formats use mathematical functions which describe curve segments using four points in a coordinate space. TrueType uses functions called quadratic splines, and PostScript uses functions called Bezier curves. The outlines are interpreted by the rasterizer, which calculates the correct bitmap to represent the outline on the device being used, whether it's a monitor or a printer.

Multiple Master

Multiple Master fonts are based on a three-dimensional matrix of primary fonts. Intermediate fonts, or *instances*, are created by interpolation between the primaries. Some Multiple Master fonts have axes for weight, width, and style, which eliminates the need for separate fonts for bold or light, extended or condensed, and italic or roman. A fourth axis, optical scaling, attempts to compensate for the fact that the eye perceives type at small sizes differently than at large sizes. When metal type was made in different sizes, the design varied subtly from size to size. This subtlety was lost with digital fonts, which use a single outline scaled to different sizes. Multiple Master fonts with built-in optical scaling give the optimum appearance at any particular size, thickening or thinning the strokes just as metal type used to.

The fifty bisected offices

The fifty bisected offices

The fifty bisected offices

TrueType GX

One feature of Apple's TrueType GX format is its automatic substitution of ligatures for specific character combinations (see the figure, Beyond the Basic Alphabet for a discussion of *ligatures*). The first line uses no ligatures; in the second line, the substitution has been made for the *ffi* combination. TrueType GX requires an operating system with QuickDraw GX.

Beyond the Basic Alphabet

!"#$%&'()*+,-./012345
6789:;<=>?@ABCDEFG
HIJKLMNOPQRSTUV
WXYZ[\]^_`abcdefghij
klmnopqrstuvwxyz{|}~
ÄÅÇÉÑÖÜáàâäãåçéèêë
íìîïñóòôöõúùûü†°¢£§•¶
ß®©™´¨ ÆØ ± ¥µ
ªº æø¿¡¬ ƒ «»…
ÀÃÕŒœ-— ""'' ÷ ÿŸ/¤‹
›fifl‡·,„‰ÂÊÁËÈÍÎÏÌÓ
Ô ÒÚÛÙ₁ˆ˜¯˘˙˚¸˝˛ˇ

Basic Character Set

The core set of characters consists of 128 characters defined by ASCII (standard character set) as well as an additional 128 characters defined by the font vendor (extended character set). Some fonts, especially display typefaces, don't use the entire 256 spaces available.

Ornaments or Dingbats

These small decorative elements can be simple—a bullet, for example—or elaborate, such as intricate ornaments that are unique to a specific typeface. Some fonts consist only of small pictures or symbols. These picture fonts may be informative, such as the symbols used in mapmaking, decorative, such as elements used to create borders; or mischievous, such as tiny faces and places used to illustrate a story.

Expert Set

An expert set is a set of fonts consisting of supplemental characters such as small caps, swashes, ligatures, old-style figures, and so on that enhance a standard font's basic character set. Often one core font will have many expert sets; one just for swash characters, another for bold swash characters, one just for small caps and old-style figures, another for bold small caps and old-style figures, and so on.

ff fi fl ffi ffl ct st

Ligatures

A combination of two letters made into a single *glyph*, or symbol, a ligature most often replaces two slim letters that benefit from close juxtaposition. Common examples are the fi and ff combinations, which are often found in the core font set, but ct and st are part of many expert sets.

1 2 3 4 5 6 7 8 9

Old-Style Figures

These alternate numerals descend below the baseline.

Typographer's Quotes

Frequently, one of the telltale signs of a "desktop published" document is the use of straight quotation marks instead of the typographer's curly quotation marks designed for that purpose

Frequently, one of the telltale signs of a "desktop published" document is the use of straight quotation marks instead of the typographer's curly quotation marks designed for that purpose

G W 2

Swashes

Swash characters flaunt fancy flourishes for their beginning or terminating strokes. Used sparingly for dramatic effect to open a chapter, start a section, or dress up an invitation.

SMALL CAPS
SMALL CAPS

Small Caps

Your page layout program gives you the option to style letters as small caps; expert sets contain true small caps. The small caps generated by page layout programs are always slightly lighter in weight than a true small cap, so full-size caps appear too heavy. With true small caps, all the characters appear the same weight.

How a Page Layout Program Works

WHAT'S THE DIFFERENCE between word processing and page layout? There's a considerable overlap between high-end word processing programs and low-end page layout programs. Most page layout programs contain word processing features such as search and replace, and most word processing programs allow you to combine type and graphics on the page. But word processing programs treat their data as a continuous stream, while page layout programs, as you might expect, use the page as their basic unit.

A page layout program's *master pages* form the basis for each page in the publication, and serve two functions. They hold repeating elements such as page numbers, borders, running heads, and rules, and they also hold nonprinting elements such as column and margin guides that form the structural underpinnings of the pages. You normally set up the master pages before flowing any text or placing any graphics into the publication.

Two levels of formatting apply to text: paragraph formats and character formats. Paragraph formats, which apply to entire paragraphs, include indents for the first line and for the left and right margins, and so on. You can also define rules above or below as part of a paragraph format. Character formats, which apply to individual characters, include font, style, size, and leading.

One of the most powerful tools for automating production is the concept of paragraph style (some programs call them style sheets). An entire set of paragraph and character formats can be stored, given a name, and applied to paragraphs of text with a keystroke or two. You can set up styles for different levels of headings, for body text, for bulleted lists, for captions, and so on.

Many word processing programs can incorporate graphics, but page layout programs provide much more power and flexibility. You can place them directly on the page, in which case the text will flow around them, or you can be anchor them to a specific location in the text. If subsequent edits cause the location to move, the anchored graphic will move with it.

You can store graphics directly inside the publication, or as external files. If you change a graphic that's stored externally, the page layout program will update it automatically.

Setting Up Documents in Page Layout Programs

Master Pages

Master pages form the structural underpinnings of a publication's pages, and hold repeating elements such as headings and page numbers.

Running heads can be set separately for left and right pages.

Column guides allow you to control the way your text flows onto the pages. For designs with facing pages, you can set inside and outside margins instead of left and right margins, so that extra room is left on the inside margins for binding.

How Desktop Publishing Works

TEXT FORMATTING

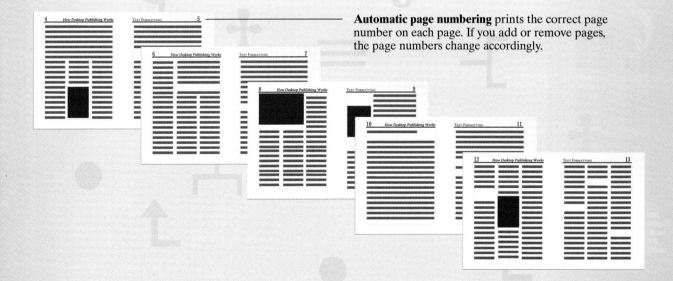

Automatic page numbering prints the correct page number on each page. If you add or remove pages, the page numbers change accordingly.

Paragraph and Character Style

Paragraph style comprises both paragraph and character formats. You can base one style upon another. For example, you can define a style for body text, then base heading styles and list styles upon it. If you need to make a global change, perhaps choosing a different font, you can simply change the definition of the body text style. The new font will automatically be applied to the heading and list styles as well as to the body text style on which these styles are based.

Local formatting overrides paragraph styles. You can, for example, italicize a word for emphasis. If you change the font used in the style definition, the italicized word will appear in the new font, but it will still be italicized.

Character fromats give you further control of your text's appearance. Attributes such as font, style, and size can be applied on a word-by-word basis or integrated into a paragraph style.

Heading style: Body text + font, bold, 13 point, 16 points leading, all caps, aligned center, first indent 0p, very loose track, column break before, 8 points space after.

Body text style: Garamond 10 point, 12 points leading, justified, normal track, first indent 0p3, 12 points space after.

Paragraph Formats

Page layout programs give you additional control over text by allowing you to set paragraphs by defining paragraph attributes. Here are some of the key paragraph formats:

First line indent applies to the first line of a paragraph.

Space before or **after** inserts a set space before or after each paragraph.

Left indent moves all text in from the left margin.

Right indent moves all text in from the right margin.

Tabs can be incorporated into a style specifically for lists.

Alignment lets you set text flush left, flush right, justified, or centered.

Word and letter spacing is set according to your column and font choice. Tracking can also be set in the paragraph formats.

FORMATTING AND STYLE SHEETS

Understanding how to use formatting and style sheets in your page layout program can save you time and frustration. They work together to make applying attributes and changes to text easy.

Two levels of formatting apply to text: paragraph formats and character formats. *How Desktop Publishing Works* defines these two types of formatting as follows:

Paragraph formats, as their name implies, apply to entire paragraphs. These include indents for the first line and for the left and right margins, alignment, word and letter spacing, and space before or after paragraphs. Character formats apply to individual characters. Font, style, size, leading, and superscript or subscript all may be applied as character formats.

Character and paragraph formats are both part of style sheets.

Style sheets help automate production. Typical attributes of a style sheet are as follows:

• Type size and style
• Indents and tabs
• Alignment

Setting up a style sheet may seem like a laborious process. But if you take the time to set it up now, making changes later will be *easy.*

List style: Body text + first indent 0p, left indent 0p3, left tab 0p3.

Leading lets you set the amount of space between lines of type.

Size simply increases or decreases point size

Style gives you bold, italic, bold italic, and so on.

Font indicates your typeface design.

How Page Layout Programs Link Graphics to the Page

Graphics can be placed directly on the page, or anchored to specific text. Graphics anchored to text move when the text moves.

You can control the text wrap for graphics placed directly on the page. An irregular text wrap runs the text around the outline of a graphic.

New Year's Calls

The genial custom of making New Year's calls has some privileges "more honored in the breach than in the observance," but there are few persons in society who would wish to abolish the time-honored license of that festive season, however strenuously they may counsel wise reforms.

The formalities enforced in polite circles at other seasons are relaxed with the coming of the New Year, and it is proper to define the privileges of the day.

Guests on their entrance to the hall are expected to remove overcoats, hats and gloves, so that they can enter the drawing room free to receive and offer salutations.

The reception-room would be warm and beautiful for the festive season. There are many forms in which refreshments may be presented with but little danger for even the weakest, and the palate is not the chief means for social delight. The veriest anchorite would prescribe refreshments for callers on New Year's Day, but some most estimable ladies in fashionable society are now favorable to the use of coffee, tea, and other harmless liquids, instead of the dangerous stimulants which a few years ago made it impossible for the caller to speak his mother tongue after he had made his calls.

When a hurried call is intended, the outer wraps may be left in the hall, and in such cases although refreshments be offered, they should not be urged.

Gloves should be retained on their right hands by gentlemen whose business and pleasure for the day will consist mainly in meeting and offering salutations to their friends. Cards must be presented by callers, and should be sent up to the reception-room while the visitors are preparing to be ushered into the presence of the ladies. Gentlemen making calls will present their cards, neatly written, engraved, or printed in script.

Calls may be made on New Year's Day as early as ten in the morning, and as late as nine at night, but before that time evidences of fatigue become common.

Carriages may be used when making calls if the round of acquaintances is large, for the purpose of saving time as well as strength, but people may walk if they wish and their calls are few. Sometimes young gentlemen who have no carriages of their own unite to hire for the occasion.

Adapted from *Gaskell's Compendium of Forms*, G. W. Borland Publishing Company, 1884

You can store graphics directly in the publication, or create a link between the publication and the source file. If you change the source file, you can automatically apply the changes in your publication.

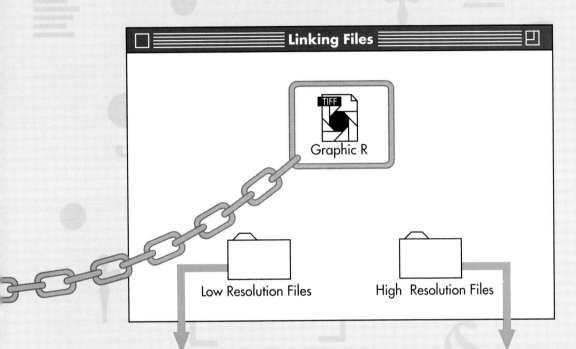

Linking Files

Graphic R

Low Resolution Files   High Resolution Files

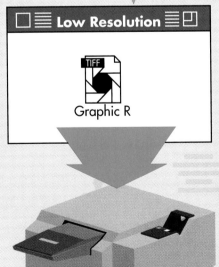

Low Resolution

Graphic R

Low-resolution graphics are smaller in data size, faster to print, and, therefore, easier to work with than high-resolution files. You can use a low-resolution version of the graphic through the proofing stages and change the link to use the high-resolution equivalent for final output.

High Resolution

Graphic R

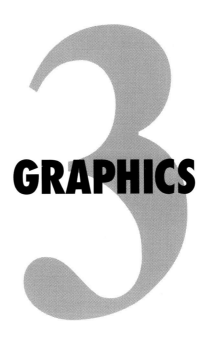

3
GRAPHICS

CONTENTS

Chapter 8: Traditional Graphics
62

Chapter 9: Computer Graphics
68

Chapter 10: How Graphics Programs Work
74

A KEY DISTINCTION between desktop publishing and its traditional counterpart is the ease and flexibility with which graphics are integrated into publications. In traditional publishing, graphics are handled separately from text in a specialized process resulting in photographic film that must be inserted into a hard-copy layout. Today's desktop publishers can drop a photographic image into an electronic layout at the click of a button, then run out the entire page in one fell swoop.

As we have seen with type, many concepts and metaphors of the traditional graphics professional carry over to desktop publishing. Before, a film stripper would literally cut a window in a film and paste photographic film into that window. Now the same results can be accomplished in a fraction of the time with Cut and Paste commands on personal computers.

Although the objectives of adding graphics to publications remain the same—to convey information visually and to add decoration—computer-generated graphics have had a profound impact on publishing. Today's newspaper or magazine editor no longer thinks strictly in terms of text, but must also consider whether information can be more effectively conveyed by graphics. The personal computer is responsible for the *infographic*, that ubiquitous hybrid of illustration and chart.

Graphics can take many forms. In fact, with desktop publishing technology, even text itself can be treated as a graphic and transformed in new and interesting ways. But before we rush headlong into the brave new world of computer graphics, it's important to understand how graphics developed over time. In Chapter 8, we'll look at the traditional approach to graphics.

The nature of graphics is directly tied to the processes that create them. We'll explore color printing in later chapters, but it's helpful to know the role printing has played in the development of the two main graphic types: line art and continuous-tone images.

Printing presses put ink on paper in tightly controlled amounts. But that's essentially all they do. Any given spot on a page is either covered with ink, or is left blank. We showed you in Chapter 1 how the halftone process using only black ink produces an illusion of shades of gray. The same process is used to print different shades, or tints, of an ink, but each color ink must be applied separately. Modern presses can print four, five, six or even more colors in a single run, but they are, essentially, several single-color presses linked together. Preparing pages for press output requires making a separate image, or *plate*, for each ink that will be used.

The methods used to produce the plates gave rise to the classifications of line art and continuous-tone image. Pen-and-ink drawings are examples of *line art* because they are composed of lines and of flat-color areas, either solid or tinted. They were traditionally reproduced using *spot colors*, where a different premixed ink is used for each color. Paintings and photographs, on the other hand, are called *continuous-tone images*, because they contain subtle, continuous gradations of color. These types of graphic elements employ *process color*, which uses only four inks—cyan, yellow, magenta, and black. When these colors are printed together, they reproduce a full range of color. In other words, a line-art illustration which calls for the color pink would be printed with pink ink; a continuous-tone image which calls for the color pink would be printed with percentages of magenta and yellow inks, yielding the color pink.

Desktop publishing has adopted the traditional classifications of line art and continuous-tone imagery, but in the translation from traditional to deskop production, the meaning of those classifications has changed. We saw in Chapter 6 that digital type can take one of two forms, bitmap or outline. In the same way, computer graphics can be classified as raster or vector. *Raster* graphics are similar to bitmaps, with the key distinction that the pixels in raster graphics, unlike those in bitmapped type, aren't limited to a single data bit of information. Instead, each pixel can contain any one of up to 16.7 million different colors. *Vector* graphics are similar to outline type. They are composed of mathematical descriptions of shapes, each of which can be assigned an outline of a given width and color, and a fill of the same or another color.

There is a natural relationship between vector graphics and line art, and between raster graphics and continuous-tone imagery, but desktop technology has blurred the once hard-and-fast distinction between line art and continuous tone as it changed the way graphic elements are created and prepared for printing. For example, with desktop publishing tools, it's easy to combine line art and continuous-tone images in the same piece of artwork. Furthermore, line art is no longer restricted to solid colors and tints— the computer has made it easier to use process color in line art than was before possible.

All the different types of computer graphics programs rely on the same fundamental building blocks that describe how images are presented on the computer screen and on the printed page. When pages are printed, the computer tells the output device where to put the marks on the page and what color to make them. Although there are several competing standards, the basic methods of specifying position and color are shared by all programs.

These building blocks are important for two reasons. They save program developers from having to reinvent the wheel each time they come out with a new program, and they provide a common language that graphics programs and page layout programs can share, allowing desktop publishers to incorporate graphics in their page layouts. The de facto standard programming language to define these mathematical descriptions is Adobe's PostScript page-description language—the printer language that gave birth to desktop publishing—which we'll discuss again when we explore desktop printing technologies. PostScript also has comprehensive graphics capabilities.

There are other standards for describing graphic shapes, such as Hewlett-Packard's Printer Control Language (PCL), which is built into every Hewlett-Packard laser printer and is in common use on the Windows platform, and Apple's QuickDraw, which is the native graphics language of the Apple Macintosh. But they both are limited in their capabilities, compared to PostScript. Unlike QuickDraw and PCL graphics, PostScript graphics are *resolution-independent*. The same PostScript file can be printed on a low-resolution laser printer and on a high-resolution imagesetter, and in each case it will print at the best quality the device can offer. PCL and QuickDraw are both as yet limited to output on desktop printers. In Chapter 9, we examine these fundamentals, looking at the various ways computers describe pages, and the way they use numbers to represent color.

There are literally hundreds of different programs for creating and manipulating graphics, but they can all be classified in terms of the kinds of work to which they are suited—line art illustrations and continuous-tone images—again echoing traditional methods. In Chapter 10, we look at the various types of computer graphics, and the kind of material to which each is suited. Then, we look at typical programs devised to work with each type, their tools and capabilities, and the ways in which the user interacts with them to create various forms of graphics.

As we'll see, desktop publishing may have adopted much of the terminology of traditional publishing, but it has extended the possibilities attainable with the old processes, and has also created some completely new types of art, such as three-dimensional modelling and rendering, which creates photorealistic images of scenes that exist only in the computer's memory.

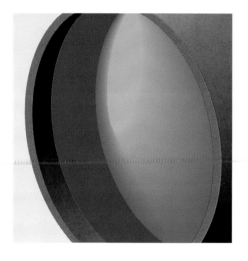

Traditional Graphics

I N TRADITIONAL PUBLISHING, the photographic process is vital to prepare both line art and continuous-tone imagery for printing, but it is used in rather different ways for each type of art. Before the introduction of the photographic process, graphics were reproduced using hand-engraved printing plates. The first examples were crude woodcuts, but over the centuries different plate materials were used, leading to the stunning work of nineteenth-century lithographers such as Currier & Ives. Their lithographs depicted continuous-tone subjects such as paintings, with as many as 40 separate plates engraved by hand. This was a labor-intensive process requiring highly skilled artisans, and hence, was very expensive. Photography transformed color printing from an art to an industrial process.

With line art, the production process often is quite separate from the creative work and could even be executed by different individuals. The creative artist produces a finished illustration using pens, brushes, and colored inks. When the illustration has been approved, the production process begins anew. The production artist must redraw the artwork using pen and ink on a transparent substrate such as mylar to create a separate overlay for each color required. The color is noted on each overlay, but the art itself is drawn in black. Where tints or screens are indicated, more overlays are called into service, using a translucent material such as Rubylith, which is cut to the exact size and shape of the area to be screened. The complete art, with all the overlays in place, is attached to a board using wax or tape; this is known as a *mechanical*. The mechanical is then delivered to the print house, where a camera operator shoots each overlay onto a separate piece of photographic paper or film, adding registration marks so that each layer of ink will register, or align, with the others. Where tints are used, the camera operator places a screen over the material being photographed, thereby creating a halftone pattern. Separate inks are used for each color.

Continuous-tone originals such as photographs are printed using process color. If you look closely at a color photograph in a magazine or book, you'll find that it's made up of a pattern of tiny dots. This pattern of dots is created by four separate halftones printed in cyan, magenta, yellow, and black. The halftones are placed at angles to each other so that, rather than simply printing one color atop the other, the inks form a regular rosette pattern.

To produce the plates from which these halftones are printed, four separate camera exposures are required, one for each color. The image to be reproduced is shot four times through different colored filters to yield four separate pieces of film called color separations. Each piece of film is halftoned at a different angle. When plates are made from the separations and the image is printed on the press, the result is a tight pattern of dots that produces the illusion of a full-color photograph.

One of the great benefits of desktop publishing is that, unlike traditional publishing, there's no absolute distinction between the creative phase and the production phase. Once the creative phase is completed, much of the production work has already been done. An illustrator working at a computer can print work on a desktop printer, then show that print to the client for approval. Once the illustration has been finalized, the same file can be sent to an imagesetter to create the spot color overlays, with any necessary screens already in place, or exported to a page layout program. Similarly, continuous-tone images can be separated electronically, retouched, color-corrected, and printed on a desktop printer for rough proofing before being sent to an imagesetter or exported as a file for placement in a page layout program.

Today, some publications still use a combination of traditional and electronic methods. Illustrations and photographs may be produced traditionally, as described above, while the layout and typographic elements are generated with desktop publishing. The page layout is printed on an imagesetter and pasted onto boards, then the graphic is cut into the layout by hand. But as the technology to produce digital graphics improves, more and more publications are taking the direct digital route.

Line Art and Continuous-Tone Images

Line art

Using pen and colored inks, an artist draws an illustration on paper. The artwork is approved, and the artist redraws the illustration outline in black on heavy paper and attaches a separate overlay for each color. When affixed to cardboard, the illustration and attached overlays are known as a *mechanical*.

At the print shop, a camera operator shoots each overlay separately. Registration marks ensure that the individual pieces of film align correctly. If tints, or shades of color, are called for, the camera operator uses a screen to diffuse color. The resulting film will be used to create printing plates—one plate for each color. Since the colored ink appears in tightly controlled areas, this printing process is known as *spot color*.

Continuous-tone image

A photographer shoots a picture, then develops and prints it. At the print shop, the camera operator shoots the photograph through four separate filters: red, blue, green, and neutral (gray) to extract color information that corresponds to cyan, magenta, yellow, and black inks, respectively. The four resulting films, called *separations,* are halftoned so each piece of film has a tight pattern of dots. The film is exposed onto four printing plates, and the photograph is printed with cyan, magenta, yellow, and black inks. These four inks used together—called *process color*—reproduce a full range of color.

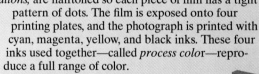

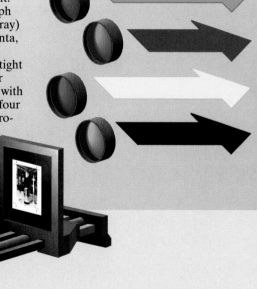

Computer Graphics

THE COMPUTER COUNTERPARTS to line-art illustrations and continuous-tone images are vector graphics and raster images. The difference between these two approaches is as clear as that between their traditional predecessors. There are also parallels between these two types of graphics and bitmap and outline fonts.

Raster images work in very much the same way bitmap fonts do—they are made up of pixels. But there's an important difference. Because bitmaps use only one bit of data to represent each pixel, they are limited to black and white, since each pixel can have only one of two values, on or off. Bitmaps, therefore, are a specialized subset of the more general class of raster images.

Raster images, on the other hand, can use up to 24 bits of data to represent each pixel. The number of bits of data used to describe a pixel is known as the *bit depth*. With 24 bits per pixel, each pixel can be any one of 16.7 million colors, rather than the black or white of a simple bitmap. In desktop publishing, the most commonly used bit depths are 1 bit, for simple monochrome graphics and text; 8 bits, for gray-scale images; and 24 bits, for full-color images.

Gray-scale images that use 8 bits per pixel can contain up to 256 shades of gray, which generally is considered sufficient to reproduce the full range of tonal values that printed material can handle. You may encounter 8-bit color, but it's useful primarily for screen display only. For full-color publishing work, 24 bits per pixel is used. The image is made up of three superimposed 8-bit channels, one each for red, green, and blue. Combining 256 levels each of red, green, and blue makes it possible for a pixel to be any one of 16.7 million colors (2^{24} = 16.7 million).

Vector graphics work quite differently than raster images. Instead of a collection of pixels, they are made up of mathematical descriptions of lines and shapes, just as outline fonts are. The graphic appears on the computer screen as a series of pixels, but its lines and shapes are made up of a series of commands that exist independently of the pixel representation.

Raster images are best suited for photo-realistic imagery, either in gray-scale or in color, which vector graphics can't handle. But raster graphics create very large files, particularly when 24-bit color is used, so vector graphics are better for most other types of illustrations, since their mathematical descriptions take up only a fraction of the space needed for raster graphics.

What Is a Raster Image?

Like your computer screen, raster images are made of pixels mapped to specific locations. Since raster images consist of color pixels adjacent to each other, they can represent the subtle, continuous gradations of color necessary to reproduce continuous-tone images. If you enlarge or rotate a raster image, its edges will appear jagged and coarse. That's because the image contains a fixed number of pixels, and enlarging it simply makes those pixels bigger. The effect is similar to creating a mosaic out of tiny square tiles. Pixels are made of bits of data (*bits* are short for *binary digits*, represented by 1 or 0). Raster image files are large, because they have to describe the location and color of each pixel.

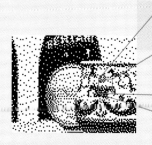

Simple black-and-white bitmaps use only 1 bit per pixel, so each pixel can be either black or white ($2^1 = 2$ shades).

Gray-scale images use 8 bits per pixel, which allows each pixel to be black, white, or any one of 254 intervening shades of gray, making a total of 256 possible values ($2^8 = 256$ shades).

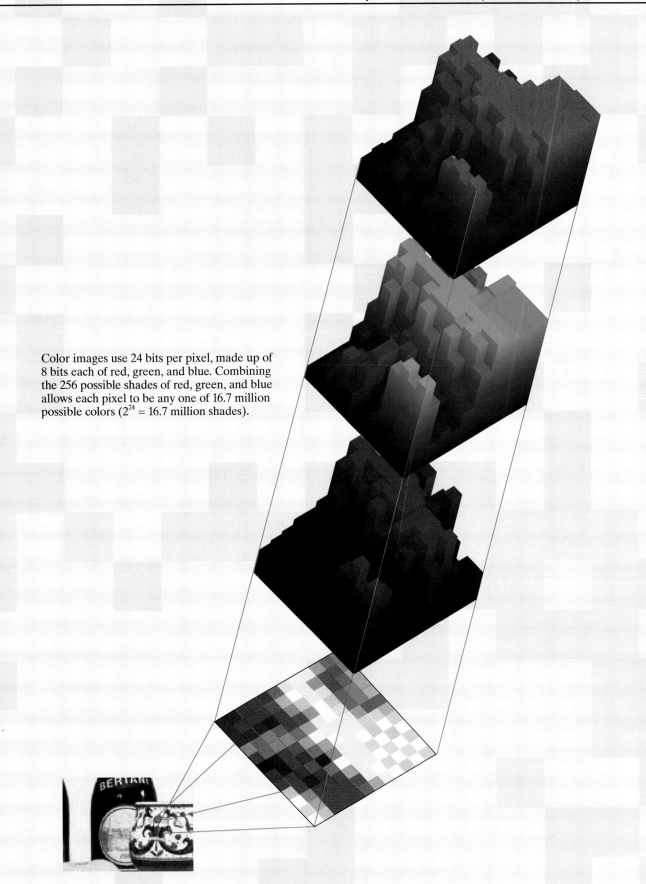

Color images use 24 bits per pixel, made up of
8 bits each of red, green, and blue. Combining
the 256 possible shades of red, green, and blue
allows each pixel to be any one of 16.7 million
possible colors (2^{24} = 16.7 million shades).

What Is a Vector Image?

Unlike raster images made up of pixels, vector graphics are made up of lines and shapes. Like traditional line art, vector graphics have a smooth, crisp quality. When you enlarge or rotate a vector graphic, its edges remain crisp and smooth. Since computer monitors and printers use pixels to represent graphics, vector art has to be rasterized (turned into dots) before you can see what it is, but the underlying mathematical data is untouched.

In PostScript illustration programs, the drawn shapes that make up vector graphics contain control points that define their curves. These points and curves are represented mathematically in a PostScript data file. Shapes can have an outline and a fill, each independent of the other.

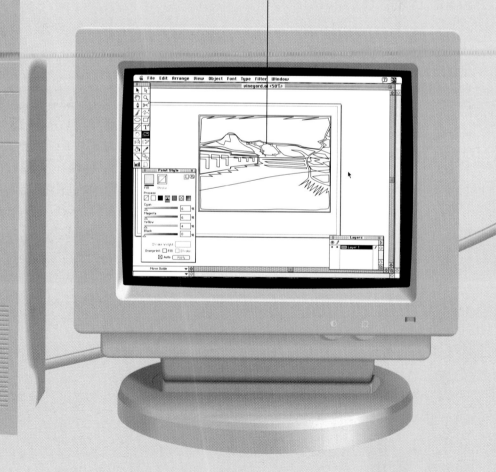

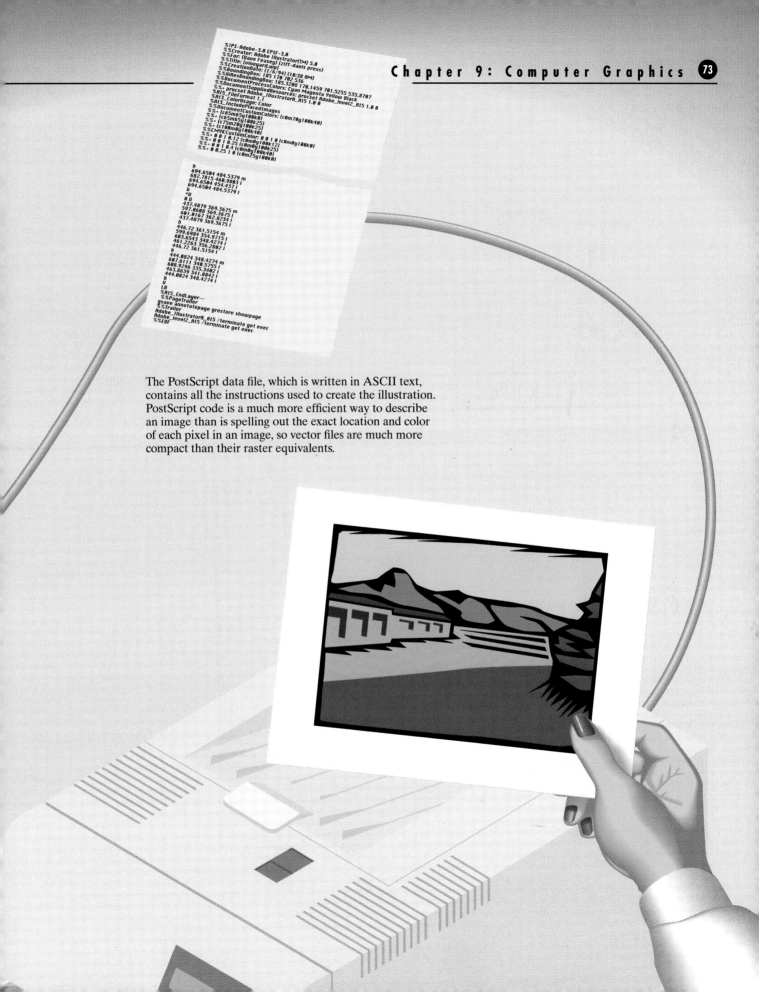

```
%!PS-Adobe-3.0 EPSF-3.0
%%Creator: Adobe Illustrator(TM) 5.0
%%For: (Dave Feasey) (ziff-davis press)
%%Title: (vineyard.wp)
%%CreationDate: (1/6/94) (10:38 AM)
%%BoundingBox: 185 170 782 536
%%HiResBoundingBox: 185.3200 170.1459 701.5255 535.8707
%%DocumentProcessColors: Cyan Magenta Yellow Black
%%DocumentSuppliedResources: procset Adobe_Illustrator_AI5 1.0 0
%%+ procset Adobe_level2_AI5 1.0 0
%AI3_ColorUsage: Color
%AI3_IncludePlacedImages
%%DocumentCustomColors: (c0m70y100k40)
%%+ (c65m65y100k0)
%%+ (c75m20y100k25)
%%+ (c100m0y100k40)
%%CMYKCustomColor: 0 0 1 0 (c0m0y100k0)
%%+ 0 0 1 0.12 (c0m0y100k12)
%%+ 0 0 1 0.25 (c0m0y100k25)
%%+ 0 0 1 0.4 (c0m0y100k40)
%%+ 0 0.25 1 0 (c0m25y100k0)
```

```
b
694.6504 484.5379 m
682.7815 460.9803 l
694.6504 454.4371 l
694.6504 484.5379 l
U
0 D
437.4879 369.3675 m
597.0600 369.3675 l
601.0167 362.8254 l
437.4879 369.3675 l
b
446.72 361.5154 m
599.6904 354.9715 l
603.6543 348.4274 l
461.2263 356.2802 l
446.72 361.5154 l
b
444.0824 348.4274 m
607.6111 348.5755 l
600.9296 335.3402 l
463.8639 341.0842 l
444.0824 348.4274 l
b
U
LB
%AI5_EndLayer--
%%PageTrailer
gsave annotatepage grestore showpage
%%Trailer
Adobe_Illustrator_AI5 /terminate get exec
Adobe_level2_AI5 /terminate get exec
%%EOF
```

The PostScript data file, which is written in ASCII text, contains all the instructions used to create the illustration. PostScript code is a much more efficient way to describe an image than is spelling out the exact location and color of each pixel in an image, so vector files are much more compact than their raster equivalents.

How Graphics Programs Work

MANY DIFFERENT GRAPHICS programs are available to today's desktop publisher, but they all fall into one of a few general categories—paint, illustration, or three-dimensional modelling. Programs in the same category share basic tools and capabilities, though each application may have its own special features. Graphics programs of interest to desktop publishers allow artists to save their work in common file formats that page layout programs accept. Pointing devices such as the mouse and the graphics tablet let the program mimic traditional graphics tools such as brushes and pens.

Paint programs and image-editing programs share many similarities. Both are raster based, and provide the digital equivalents of traditional painting tools such as variable-sized brushes, airbrushes, even paint buckets. Image-editing programs usually contain the full complement of painting tools, but also include special tools for altering scanned images, such as brightness, contrast, and sharpening controls. They also let the artist use a scanner to capture photographic images directly into the program. Image-editing programs serve as the digital equivalent of a photographer's darkroom.

Illustration programs are vector based, and most are based on the PostScript page-description language. Working with PostScript-based illustration programs is quite different from working with painting programs. PostScript illustration consists of overlaying opaque shapes, known as *paths*, on one another—it's like creating artwork using colored paper cutouts. The tools offered by illustration programs are primarily concerned with creating and manipulating paths.

With three-dimensional modelling and rendering programs, the artist creates three-dimensional models that can be viewed and lit from any angle, just as in the real world outside the computer. These programs contain aspects of both vector and raster graphics, and use two separate modules, one for modelling and one for rendering. Using the modelling component, the artist creates a wire-frame representation of the three-dimensional object that can be viewed from a variety of angles. The rendering module turns the three-dimensional wire frame into a photorealistic image, seen from a specific viewpoint. The same wire frame can be rendered from numerous different angles, using different lighting and surface textures.

How Paint and Image-Editing Programs Work

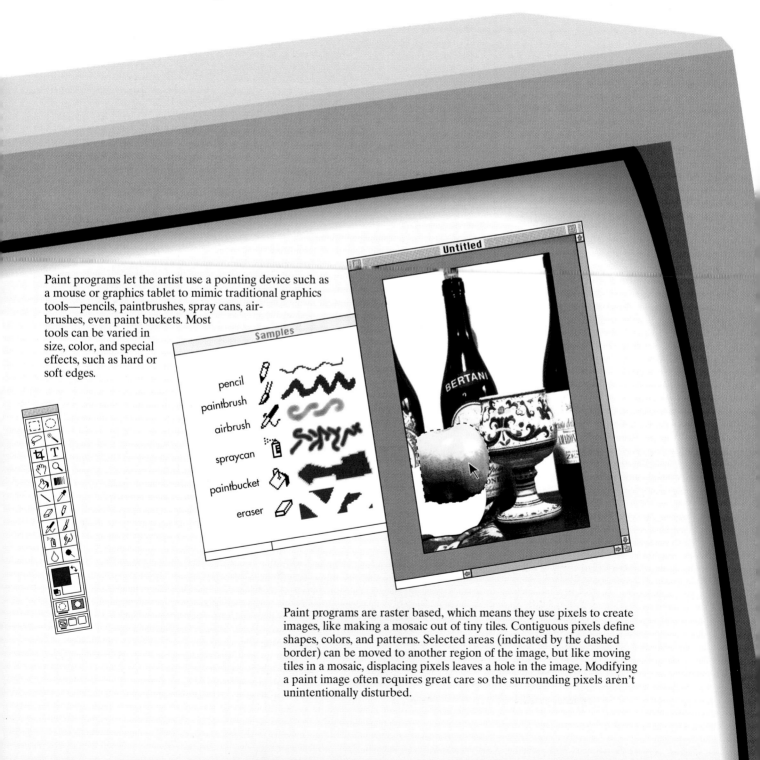

Paint programs let the artist use a pointing device such as a mouse or graphics tablet to mimic traditional graphics tools—pencils, paintbrushes, spray cans, airbrushes, even paint buckets. Most tools can be varied in size, color, and special effects, such as hard or soft edges.

Samples

pencil

paintbrush

airbrush

spraycan

paintbucket

eraser

Paint programs are raster based, which means they use pixels to create images, like making a mosaic out of tiny tiles. Contiguous pixels define shapes, colors, and patterns. Selected areas (indicated by the dashed border) can be moved to another region of the image, but like moving tiles in a mosaic, displacing pixels leaves a hole in the image. Modifying a paint image often requires great care so the surrounding pixels aren't unintentionally disturbed.

Image-editing programs are similar to paint programs, but they also contain controls for adjusting color balance, contrast, and brightness, and tools for creating special effects such as ripples, waves, embossing, and so on. Because they're frequently used to modify scanned pictures, image editing applications are the digital equivalent of the photographer's darkroom.

Increase saturation

Brighten

Darken

Sharpen

Increase contrast

Decrease contrast

Change color balance

Radial blur

Diffuse

Find edges

Solarize

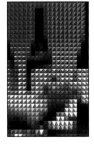

Extrude pyramids

Pointillize

Emboss

How Illustration Programs Work

PostScript illustration programs let the artist build illustrations using opaque shapes that are assembled in layers. These shapes can be easily disassembled, moved, then reassembled again without disturbing the underlying or adjacent shapes.

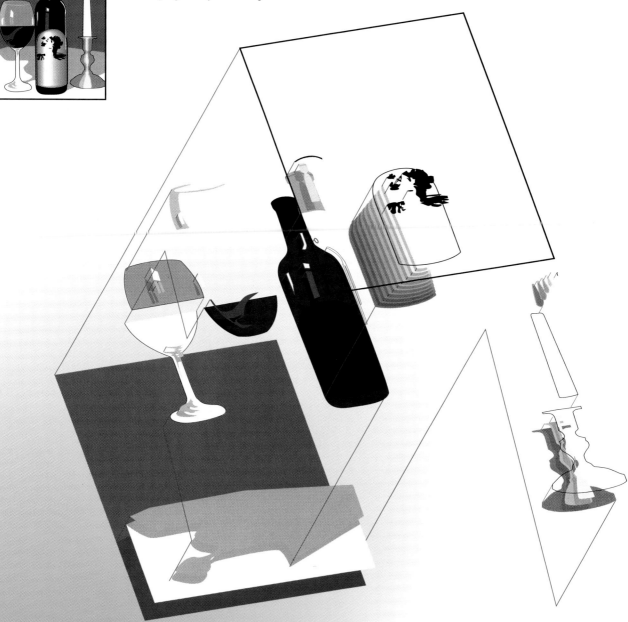

These shapes, called paths, can be closed, forming a solid shape, or open, making a simple line. Clipping paths are the inverse of normal paths, similar to holes punched in the colored paper to reveal whatever lies behind it.

Illustration programs draw from a different set of tools than do paint programs. Illustration tools are designed for drawing precise lines. Paths are drawn with a pen tool, which places points at key junctures in the lines. Anchor points are placed between line segments; control points dictate the direction and curve of the lines. Moving either point changes the shape of the path. Simple lines can also be drawn with a freehand tool. To precisely trim or segment lines, the artist turns to the digital X-ACTO blade, the knife tool.

Pen

Knife

Freehand tool

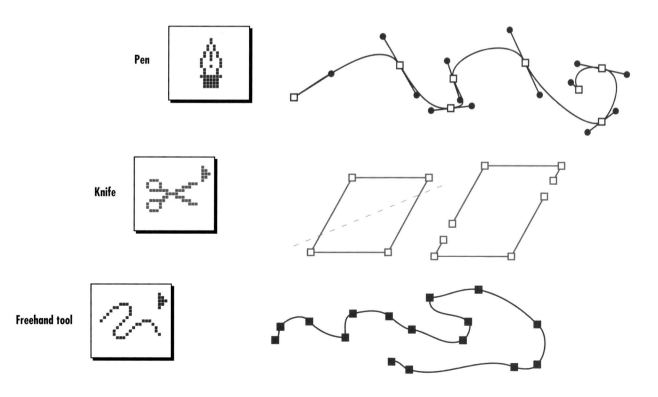

How Three-Dimensional Graphics Programs Work

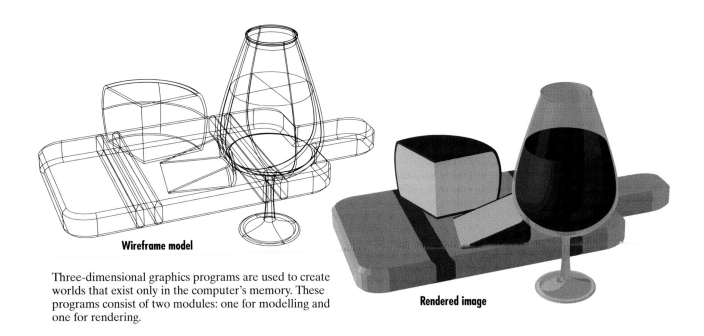

Wireframe model

Rendered image

Three-dimensional graphics programs are used to create worlds that exist only in the computer's memory. These programs consist of two modules: one for modelling and one for rendering.

The modelling component allows the artist to create a wire-frame representation of the world, similar to a skeleton, which will later be draped in clothing. The artist assembles the scene with basic shapes, called primitives. Other shapes are fashioned with specific tools that *lathe* (rotate a flat shape 360 degrees to create a solid object) or *extrude* (extend a flat shape to a third dimension) objects, techniques that add dimension to lines and shapes as defined by the artist. Individual shapes are grouped together to form objects.

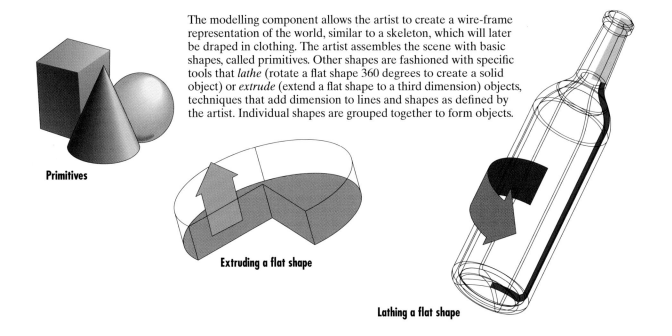

Primitives

Extruding a flat shape

Lathing a flat shape

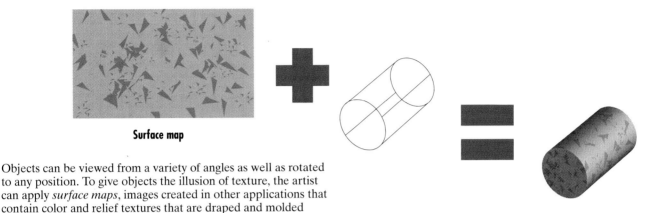

Surface map

Objects can be viewed from a variety of angles as well as rotated to any position. To give objects the illusion of texture, the artist can apply *surface maps*, images created in other applications that contain color and relief textures that are draped and molded around the wire-frame model.

Once the individual objects are complete, the artist composites them into a scene, adjusting angles, directing light sources, and applying additional surface maps. When the scene's set, rendering begins. Rendering computes all the angles, lights, colors, and patterns in the scene and transforms them into a smooth, glossy, photorealistic image. Because three-dimensional images are so complex, rendering may tie up the computer for a long time, so three-dimensional programs have the option of low-resolution previews for checking the scene in progress before final high-resolution rendering takes place. Sophisticated images may take days to render.

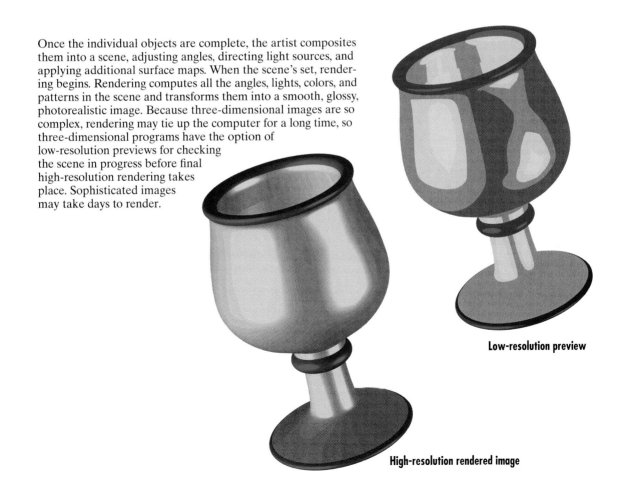

Low-resolution preview

High-resolution rendered image

COLOR

CONTENTS

Chapter 11: What Is Color?
86

Chapter 12: Printed Color
94

Chapter 13: Computer Color
100

ONE OF THE biggest changes that desktop publishing has wrought on the publishing world is the increased use of color. Color publishing has never been more affordable or more in demand than it is today. Color images and infographics enliven the formerly staid, gray pages of our newspapers. Complex color effects such as graduated blends of color, which would have been difficult if not impossible to achieve by traditional means, are now commonplace in today's publications.

However, printing color can be very complex, and color publishing is fraught with pitfalls for the unwary. One of the great benefits of desktop publishing is the much-touted WYSIWYG—What You See Is What You Get—capability of desktop publishing systems, where what you see on the screen exactly matches what you get on the printed page. Unfortunately, the concept of WYSIWYG tends to break down very quickly in the realm of color.

It is possible with a great deal of work and considerable expense to build a calibrated system, where the color performance of each device—monitor, scanner, desktop printer, and the press itself—is carefully measured, and the devices are fine-tuned to deliver consistent color matching throughout the production chain. But at present this is the exception rather than the rule. On most systems, the color you see on the screen will rarely match the color produced by a desktop color printer, which in turn is unlikely to match the color produced by the printing press.

To understand why color varies so, you need to first understand the nature of color itself. In Chapter 11, we discuss color fundamentals, paying particular attention to those ways of thinking about color that apply to desktop publishing. We look at the various ways we can represent color in order to reproduce it on different devices, and examine the fundamental difference between colored light, used by monitors and scanners, and colored pigments, used by printing presses and desktop printers.

Color printing is part art, part craft, and part science. You don't have to master press techniques in order to produce color pages, but a basic understanding of how color printing works can save you hours of frustration, not to mention expensive mistakes later on. In Chapter 12, we look at the techniques used for printing color, and the necessary compromises that they entail. We look further into the halftone process in printing, where the illusion of different shades or degrees of brightness of a single ink is produced by using a regularly spaced pattern of variable-sized dots.

As we saw in Chapter 8, color printing has traditionally used two quite separate methods, spot color and process color, to render color on the printed page. With desktop publishing technology, the distinction between the two sometimes becomes blurred, with unfortunate results. We look at the various ways desktop publishing programs let you specify color, and we point out which approach is appropriate for each printing method. We also look at the differences between printing color on a printing press and printing color on a desktop color printer.

One of the major sources of difficulty in color publishing is that computers don't really understand color. All they do is crunch numbers. As we'll see in Chapter 13, the meaning of the numbers that computers use to represent color can change according to the context. We'll look at how computers represent color, and how a single set of color values can result in quite different colors on monitors, scanners, and printers.

Furthermore, the range of colors that can be captured by scanners and displayed on the screen is greater than that which can be printed on the page using process color. We'll look at the problems involved in translating colored light into the closest possible equivalent colors of pigment needed to reproduce color on the printed page, and we'll explain some of the latest solutions to these problems.

If color publishing sounds complex, that's because it is, and we'd be doing the reader a disservice were we to pretend otherwise. But today's desktop publishing tools are making color publishing easier, more predictable, more accessible, and cheaper than ever before. It isn't necessary to use full-color photographs or complex blends to create publications with impact. One or two well-chosen spot colors, when handled well, can create the impression of many more colors than are actually used.

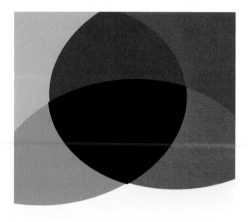

What Is Color?

WHEN YOU WERE a youngster, you were taught that red, yellow, and blue are the primary colors and that the secondary colors—orange, green, and purple—can be made by combining two primaries. If you were an attentive student, you learned that you could make tertiary colors by mixing a primary and a secondary color. Well, forget all that, because it will only confuse you. That isn't how color works when it's displayed on the computer monitor or printed on the page.

There are really two sets of primary colors, the *additive primary colors* (red, green, and blue) and the *subtractive primary colors* (cyan, magenta, and yellow). We use the additive primaries for *transmissive* color, where light shines through an object, as when we display an image on a TV screen or computer monitor, or project a transparency; and we use the subtractive primaries for *reflective* color, where light is reflected from an object such as a printed page or a photographic print.

Sir Isaac Newton discovered that white light could be split into red, green, and blue components using a prism. We call red, green, and blue the additive primary colors because we can start with black, the absence of light, and add various proportions of red, green and blue to produce all other colors. Adding together 100 percent of red, green, and blue produces white light.

Pigments such as those in printing inks work by reflecting some wavelengths of light and absorbing or subtracting others, so reflective color is the exact opposite of transmissive color. Cyan, magenta and yellow are called the subtractive primary colors because, when there are no pigments, all wavelengths of light are reflected, producing white light. We create colors by adding different proportions of cyan, magenta, and yellow. Adding 100 percent each of cyan, magenta, and yellow produces black.

Although the additive and subtractive primaries describe two alternative methods for producing color, they don't describe color itself. Color is something that happens only inside our heads. It's the human visual response to certain wavelengths of light hitting the retina. The color that we see depends on the light source, the object that we're viewing, and the sensitivity of our eyes.

A better model of color, as we experience it, describes colors in terms of three components: hue, saturation, and brightness. These three components define a *color space*, a three-dimensional model where one spatial axis represents hue, the second represents saturation, and the third represents brightness.

Hue is the property we refer to when we call a color by its name—red, purple, orange, green. *Saturation* is the degree of purity or intensity of a given color. The more gray you add to a color, the less saturated it becomes. If you remove all saturation from a color, you get a neutral gray. *Brightness* indicates how light or dark a color is, or how close it is to black or white. If you remove all the brightness, you get black.

Additive and Subtractive Colors

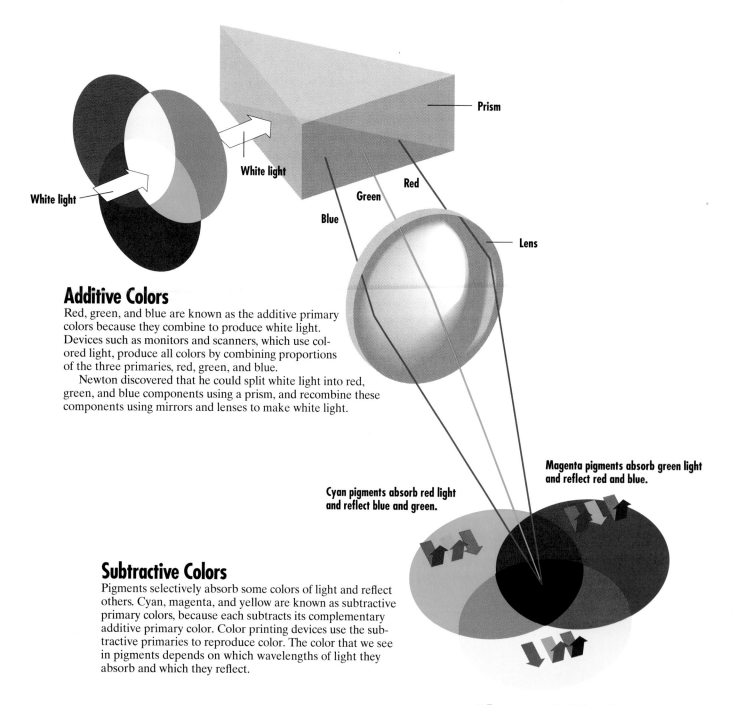

Prism

White light

Red

Green

Blue

White light

Lens

Additive Colors

Red, green, and blue are known as the additive primary colors because they combine to produce white light. Devices such as monitors and scanners, which use colored light, produce all colors by combining proportions of the three primaries, red, green, and blue.

Newton discovered that he could split white light into red, green, and blue components using a prism, and recombine these components using mirrors and lenses to make white light.

Magenta pigments absorb green light and reflect red and blue.

Cyan pigments absorb red light and reflect blue and green.

Subtractive Colors

Pigments selectively absorb some colors of light and reflect others. Cyan, magenta, and yellow are known as subtractive primary colors, because each subtracts its complementary additive primary color. Color printing devices use the subtractive primaries to reproduce color. The color that we see in pigments depends on which wavelengths of light they absorb and which they reflect.

Yellow pigments absorb blue light and reflect red and green.

Color Context

Our perception of colors is strongly affected by the context in which we view them, as these examples show. When you design with color, it's important to remember the effect that context may have on a color. A pure color viewed against a background of the same hue looks quite different when placed on a background of its complementary color.

A color appears lighter when viewed against a dark background than it does when viewed against a light background.

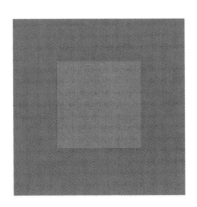

Two colors may appear similiar when viewed against different backgrounds, yet look very different when placed against the same background.

Color Spaces

Hue, Saturation, Brightness

All colors can be described in terms of hue, saturation, and brightness as the three axes of a three-dimensional space. The most common representation of the color space is shaped like two cones joined at their bases. The hues are arranged radially about the center. Saturation increases with distance from the center axis, and brightness increases as you travel up the vertical axis. If you start at the midpoint and add brightness, the range of possible saturation decreases, until you reach pure white at one apex. If you remove brightness, you eventually end up with black at the other apex.

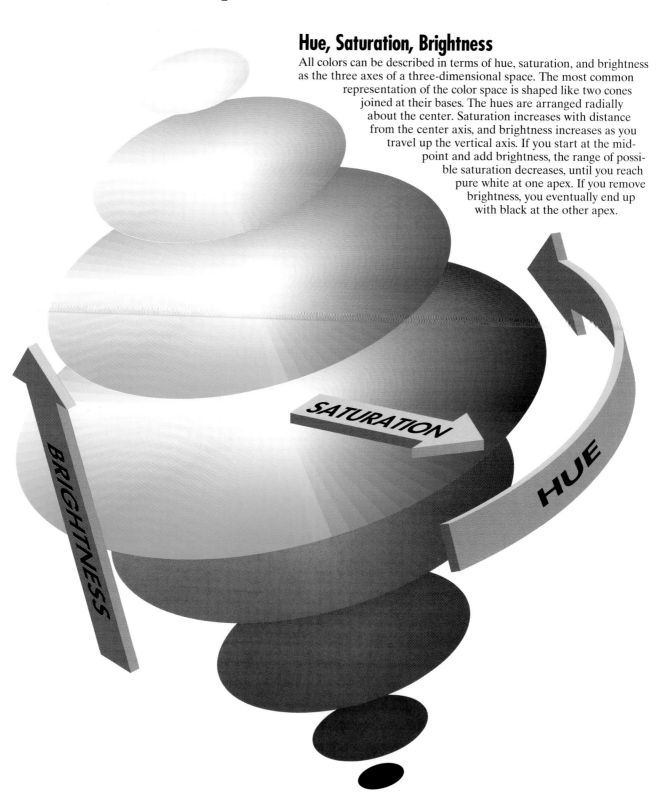

The Color Wheel

Another common representation is the color wheel. This wheel shows
a cross-section of the color space, omitting brightness, with the hues
arranged around the wheel, and saturation increasing with the distance
from the center of the wheel. Hues that lie directly opposite each other
on the wheel are known as *complementary* colors.

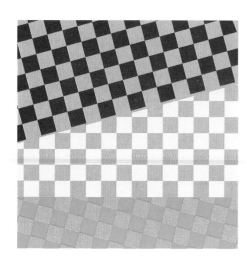

Printed Color

AS WE SAW in Chapter 8, two different methods are used to print color on the press, spot color and process color. With spot color, each color on the page is printed using a different premixed ink to produce precisely the desired color. The artist specifies a color according to a numbered selection of inks made by a vendor, such as Pantone. Spot color is usually used in two- or three-color jobs, or is added to process color in premium five-color jobs.

In process color, all the colors on the page are printed using only four inks, cyan, magenta, yellow, and black, abbreviated to CMYK. As discussed in Chapter 11, cyan, magenta, and yellow are subtractive primary colors; adding 100 percent of each produces black. So why is black ink necessary? Well, inks must have many other properties besides color. They must have the right viscosity—if they're too thick they'll gum up the press, and if they're too thin, they'll spread too much. They must dry in a reasonable amount of time, and they must be able to adhere to one another. Inks available today satisfy all these requirements, but at the cost of color purity. Combining 100 percent each of cyan, magenta, and yellow inks produces a muddy brown instead of black, so black is added as a fourth ink.

The halftone is used in both printing processes. With spot colors, the halftone process is used to create tints. This has the same effect as adding more white to the color, but the advantage of using a halftone screen is that you can produce all the tints you want using the same ink, so that the paper has to run only once through the press. With process color, the halftone process plays a more complex and important role. Each of the four process inks is printed using the same halftone screen. But if all the inks were simply printed one on top of the other, the result would be a muddy mess. So instead, the halftone for each ink is printed at a different angle.

Desktop color printers generally use either three colors—cyan, magenta, and yellow—or all four process colors. Although some desktop printers claim the ability to simulate spot colors, remember that it's only a simulation.

Many desktop publishing programs will also let you specify a spot color, and then convert it to process color. The results are almost always disappointing. If you're working with process color, specify your colors as percentages of CMYK.

How Spot Color Works

Spot-color printing requires inks that are premixed to a specific color. Artists select colors from a swatch book that shows inks by color and identifies them by number. Many color desktop publishing programs incorporate these spot-color libraries so artists can call up the same numbered colors in their illustration or layout programs.

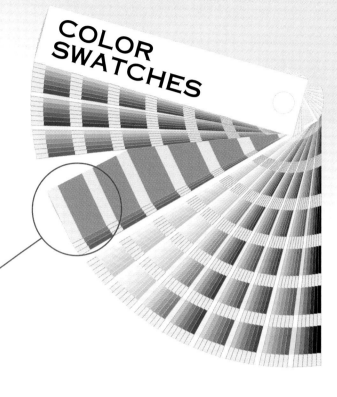

At the printing plant, an inked roller with the specified color applies the color to the page. Since spot-color printing can be costly, desktop publishers expand their range of possible colors by using tints of the same color. *Tints* are spot-color halftones in which all the dots are the same size. The screening process introduces white (actually, the color of the paper the page is printed on) into the color to produce different shades. A wide variety of tones can be produced this way. Using tints in a two- or three-color job can create the illusion of many more colors while keeping the printing bill low.

9-C
6.0 green•1.5 red•1.0 black

1-A

6-A

One often-overlooked use of spot color is the duotone, where a black-and-white photograph is reproduced using two inks rather than one. One ink, usually black, is concentrated in the shadows and midtones, while the other lighter ink carries most of the highlight detail. The resulting reproduction carries greater detail in both the dark and light areas than can be attained by printing with a single ink.

How Process Color Works

Process color printing uses cyan, magenta, yellow, and black inks to produce the full range of colors. When you pick a color in your desktop publishing program, you can set it to tell you the percentages of CMYK for that color. For example, 100 percent yellow and 100 percent magenta produce a strong red.

85 lpi

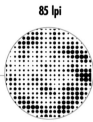

133 lpi

150 lpi

When printing a process color, each color first goes through the halftone process, from which four sets of variable-sized dots result (on your desktop printer, colors go through a process called dithering, which is a simplified way of achieving the same result). The dots vary in size to simulate different brightness values, but the spacing of the dots remains constant. This pattern is called a halftone screen, because when the technique was first introduced, it was done by photographing the subject through a mesh screen. The distance between dot centers, measured in lines per inch, is called the *screen frequency*.

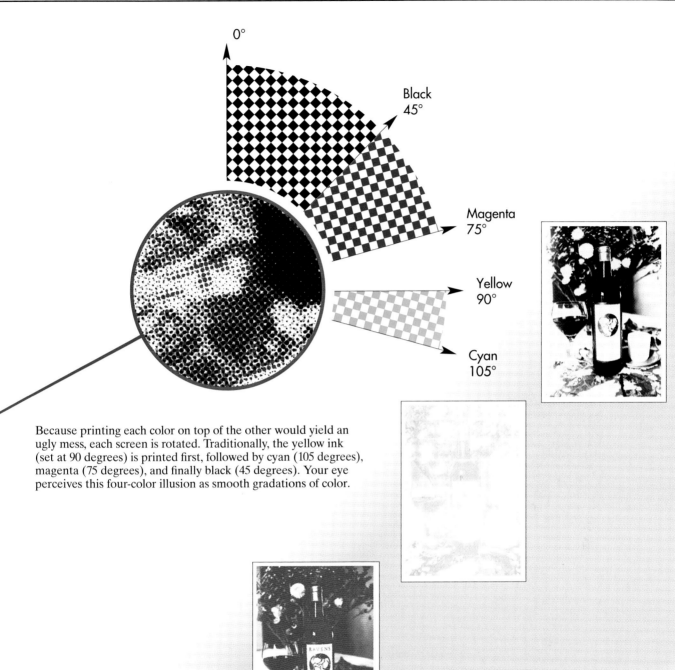

Because printing each color on top of the other would yield an ugly mess, each screen is rotated. Traditionally, the yellow ink (set at 90 degrees) is printed first, followed by cyan (105 degrees), magenta (75 degrees), and finally black (45 degrees). Your eye perceives this four-color illusion as smooth gradations of color.

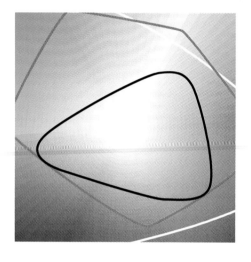

Computer Color

W E'VE SEEN THAT the printing process produces color using either custom-mixed spot inks or percentages of CMYK process-color inks. But the computer monitor displays color using varying levels of red, green, and blue light. This color model is abbreviated to RGB, and it's the native color model used in computers. It's also the color model used by most desktop scanners since, like monitors, they deal with colored light.

Part of the problem of inconsistent color between scanner, monitor, and print lies in the fact that RGB color must be translated into CMYK color before it's printed. Translating RGB to CMY is simple, but when some proportion of C, M, and Y is replaced by black, as it is in CMYK, it becomes more difficult. There are many equally valid CMYK equivalents for a given RGB value.

There's also a deeper problem. Color models like RGB and CMYK don't really represent color as such. Rather, they're recipes that a particular device such as a monitor or printer uses to produce color. Two cooks given the same recipe will often turn out rather different dishes, and the same is unfortunately true with desktop publishing devices like monitors and printers.

Monitor screens use special materials called phosphors that glow and emit light when bombarded with electrons, producing the pictures we see on the screen. Color monitors use three kinds of phosphors that emit red, green, and blue light. But different monitor vendors use different phosphors, so the same RGB values will produce slightly different colors on different monitors. The phosphors also change over the course of time, which can further alter the color.

CMYK inks are also subject to some variation—the inks used in Europe are different from those used in the Americas, and different again from those used in Asia. But the paper stock has an even greater impact on the final color. With desktop printers, the range of variation is great because different vendors and different printer technologies each use their own set of pigments.

The problem, in a nutshell, is that RGB and CMYK color specifications have a precise color meaning only in the context of a specific device. If you send those same values to another device, you'll get a different color. Desktop publishers contend with this problem every day.

Fortunately, a solution is in sight. What if, instead of specifying color in terms of the values that a particular device needs to produce a color, we could specify it in absolute terms? Well, we can, thanks to pioneering work done in the 1930s by the Commission Internationale de l'Éclairage, the international standards body that deals with illumination. The commission developed a series of color spaces that specify color as it's experienced by humans; this is known as the CIE color spaces.

In a process known as characterization, vendors can describe the actual performance of their color devices in terms of the CIE color spaces, so that each RGB or CMYK value has a known CIE equivalent. Using this information, special software known as a color management system can calculate the transformations necessary to keep color consistent throughout the whole production chain. These systems are still in their infancy, but we expect that in a few years, the problem of color consistency in desktop publishing systems will have largely vanished.

Color-Management Systems

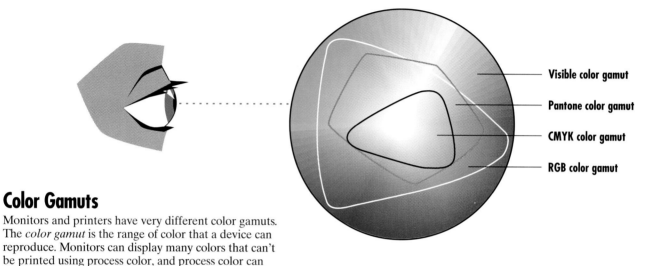

Visible color gamut

Pantone color gamut

CMYK color gamut

RGB color gamut

Color Gamuts

Monitors and printers have very different color gamuts. The *color gamut* is the range of color that a device can reproduce. Monitors can display many colors that can't be printed using process color, and process color can print a smaller number of colors that can't be displayed on the monitor.

Each device in the production chain interprets RGB and CMYK values differently, resulting in inconsistent color.

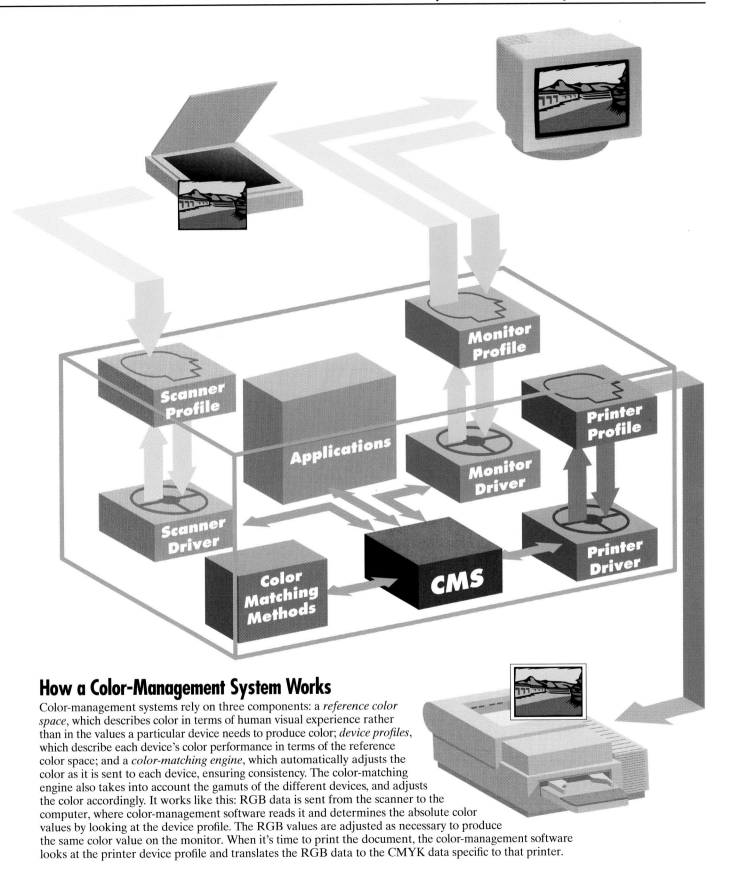

How a Color-Management System Works

Color-management systems rely on three components: a *reference color space*, which describes color in terms of human visual experience rather than in the values a particular device needs to produce color; *device profiles*, which describe each device's color performance in terms of the reference color space; and a *color-matching engine*, which automatically adjusts the color as it is sent to each device, ensuring consistency. The color-matching engine also takes into account the gamuts of the different devices, and adjusts the color accordingly. It works like this: RGB data is sent from the scanner to the computer, where color-management software reads it and determines the absolute color values by looking at the device profile. The RGB values are adjusted as necessary to produce the same color value on the monitor. When it's time to print the document, the color-management software looks at the printer device profile and translates the RGB data to the CMYK data specific to that printer.

HARDWARE

CONTENTS

Chapter 14: How Scanners Work
112

Chapter 15: How Graphic Input Devices Work
120

Chapter 16: How Storage Devices Work
128

Chapter 17: How Printers Work
132

THE BIGGEST CAPITAL expense you'll encounter in desktop publishing is the hardware that's needed to run the software we've already discussed. But bear in mind that money spent up-front can lead to savings down the road. It's possible to do desktop publishing without all the hardware devices that we describe here, but the more pieces of the production process you have under your individual control, the more flexibility you have. In figuring out the real cost of hardware, you should pay attention to the cost of owning the equipment, not just the initial capital expenditure. If you save a few hundred dollars by buying a slower computer instead of a fast one, and then find that it takes you twice as long to do your work, you probably haven't really saved anything at all.

Some hardware components can be considered optional—graphics tablets or CD-ROM drives, for instance. But desktop printers and scanners are now so inexpensive that it makes sense to buy one of each if you plan to do a lot of desktop publishing.

Of course, the one piece that's essential is a computer. In Chapter 3, we outlined a basic computer configuration that consisted of the following: a WYSIWYG operating system, such as Macintosh or Windows; the fastest processor you can afford (minimally a 68040 on the Mac and a 486 on the PC); the most memory (RAM) you can afford; and the biggest hard drive you can afford (no less than 100 megabytes). As for a monitor, a high-resolution gray-scale or color monitor is mandatory. Purchase as large a monitor as you can afford. With a large-screen monitor, you can see more than one page at a time; with a small screen, you'll spend a frustrating amount of time scrolling around when you want to work on two-page spreads at close to actual size or when you want to appraise a large graphic.

Although these pieces are critical to the desktop publishing process, we're not going to explore their inner workings—many general computer books have been written on the subject, such as *How Computers Work* and *How Macs Work* (Ziff-Davis Press). Instead, we'll look at hardware that is specifically designed for desktop publishing. These components are called peripherals, since they're outside the main CPU, but as you'll see, their functionality is not peripheral but central to the publishing process. We'll look at three different types of peripherals. *Input devices* let you bring information into the computer. *Storage devices* provide a place to store that information and, in many cases, also offer a means of transporting that information. *Output devices* let you retrieve the information stored in the computer in a readable form.

Scanners are particularly useful input devices for desktop publishers. They bring images into the computer in the form of raster or bitmap data. As we explain in Chapter 14, three main types of scanners are used for desktop publishing: desktop flatbed, desktop slide, and drum scanners. (Hand-held scanners are popular, but their small scanning area makes them ill-suited for most desktop publishing applications.) Depending on your needs, you may use any or all of these devices, but drum scanners are too costly for most operations. If you plan to print your publication on high-quality paper on a printing press, then you may want to take your images to a professional print shop or service bureau where they use drum scanners. A new breed of desktop drum scanners is becoming available, but they're still quite pricey and require a higher level of expertise to operate than do other desktop units.

As we'll see in Chapter 15, other input devices specific to desktop publishing include graphics tablets and digital cameras. Graphics tablets let you create and enter graphics by sketching with a stylus on an electronic pad. You get immediate feedback by watching the screen. Digital cameras let you take photographs, but instead of capturing images on film, they use digital media—an internal floppy disk, hard disk, or memory card. There's no need for scanning since the image is already in digital format. A hybrid approach to digital photography is the Photo CD system. Developed by Eastman Kodak Company, the Photo CD system means that you can take pictures with your own 35-millimeter camera and ask the photofinisher to supply you with a Photo CD-ROM disc as well as with the usual prints and negatives. The images on the disc are ready to be incorporated into your electronic page layout.

Of course, you need someplace to store these images. Hard disks and floppy disks are essential to any computer system, but desktop publishing also takes advantage of various specialized storage media that we describe in Chapter 16. Known as removable media, they consist of a drive mechanism and interchangeable disks, cartridges, or cassettes. They don't provide a substitute for conventional storage on hard disks, but they serve as a valuable adjunct that gives you access to unlimited amounts of storage, and allows you to transport your data easily. SyQuest and Bernoulli cartridges, magneto-optical discs, CD-ROM discs, and DAT (digital audio tape) cassettes each have their strengths and weaknesses for different purposes.

Finally, the proof of all your work appears on the printed page, so in Chapter 17, we look at printers (not the people, but the hardware). Today's desktop printing devices run the gamut from low-cost monochrome ink-jet printers to costly color dye-sublimation printers. Each type of printer can be used for a variety of activities, but again, different printers tend to excel at different applications. For printing proof pages as well as for producing camera-ready copy that can be run off on a photocopying machine, laser printers offer high quality at a reasonable price—you can find good black-and-white units for less than $1,000 (back when we started desktop publishing, laser printers cost around $7,000!). We don't include dot-matrix printers because they are simply too coarse to adequately represent the detailed typography and complex graphics required for desktop publishing.

As with drum scanners, it's unlikely that you'll purchase your own imagesetter, but if you plan to have your publication printed by a professional print shop, you need to know how imagesetters produce high-resolution film negatives and positives.

PART FIVE

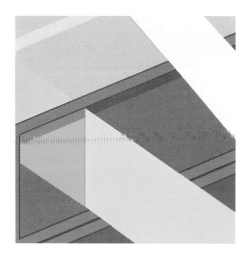

CHAPTER
14

How Scanners Work

SCANNERS ARE YOUR computer's eyes. These devices turn photographs, transparencies, and printed art into raster images on the computer. In publishing, three types of scanner are in common use: flatbed scanners, transparency scanners, and drum scanners. *Flatbed scanners* are generally the least expensive of the three, and are designed to scan reflective material such as photographic prints and printed pages. *Transparency scanners*, as their name implies, are designed for scanning photographic transparencies such as slides. Some handle only 35-millimeter format, and others can scan transparencies up to 4-by-5 inches. Since they cannot scan flat art, buy them only if you plan to scan slides exclusively. *Drum scanners* are the most expensive of the three, and also require the most skill to operate, so they're generally found only in high-end prepress shops. Drum scanners can scan either reflective or transmissive originals.

Flatbed scanners are similar to photocopying machines. Reflective art or copy (pages from a book, for example) is placed facedown on the glass bed of the scanner, where a light source illuminates it. The light that is reflected from the artwork is then directed by a combination of mirrors and lenses to a set of photosensors called CCDs, or charge-coupled devices. The CCDs are arranged in a strip, or *array*. Each element in the CCD array is a photosensor that converts light into electricity. The amount of electricity that the photosensor generates is proportional to the amount of light it receives. The electricity from the CCD is fed to an analog-to-digital converter, which turns the voltages into digital values that represent the tonal value or color of each pixel.

The CCD array, the light source, and the focusing lens form an assembly called the scanning head. A stepper motor moves the scanning head in small increments down the length of the platen, building the image one row of pixels at a time to form a gray-scale image. For color scanning, three separate gray-scale images are captured through color filters, one red, one green, and one blue, and are then combined to make a full-color RGB image. In some scanners, the scanning head makes three separate passes across the image to create the color scan; in others, the scan is made in a single pass by rotating each of the filters in front of the light source in turn.

Transparency scanners work in a similar fashion, except that the light source is placed on the opposite side of the transparency from the CCD array. Rather than moving the light source and the CCD array, the stepper motor moves the transparency itself, while the light source and CCD array remain stationary.

In a drum scanner, the original artwork to be scanned is mounted on a drum, which then rotates rapidly beneath a light source and tube-based photoreceptors known as photomultiplier tubes (PMTs). Drum scanners usually contain dedicated computers that convert the RGB image to CMYK, ready for printing.

PMT-based drum scanners generally provide the highest-quality scans, although some of the more expensive CCD-based scanners are beginning to rival that quality. But low-end scanners are useful for making rough for-position-only scans, and for scanning pencil sketches that can be translated into vector art.

Flatbed and Transparency Scanners

The light source illuminates the artwork to be scanned. The light is then directed through an optical train comprised of mirrors and lenses to the CCD array, which converts the varying levels of light into varying voltages of electricity. The analog-to-digital converter turns the voltages from the CCD array into digital values that correspond to image pixels. The CCD array captures an entire row of image pixels. The stepper motor moves the scanning head (on flatbed scanners) or the transparency (on transparency scanners) in minute increments. Each increment allows the CCD array to capture a new row of image pixels, so the image is built up row by row. Color filters are used for color scanning. The color image is made up of three superimposed planes: one red, one green, and one blue.

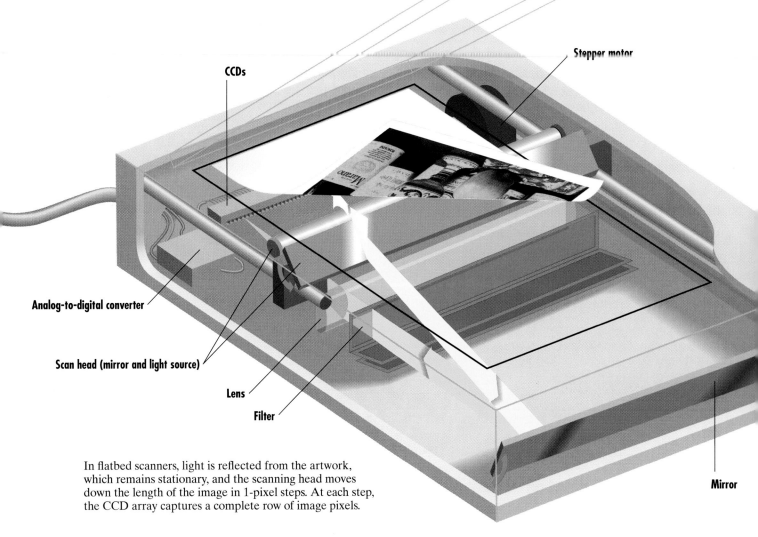

CCDs

Stepper motor

Analog-to-digital converter

Scan head (mirror and light source)

Lens

Filter

Mirror

In flatbed scanners, light is reflected from the artwork, which remains stationary, and the scanning head moves down the length of the image in 1-pixel steps. At each step, the CCD array captures a complete row of image pixels.

In transparency scanners, the light shines through the artwork. The light source and CCD array remain stationary, and the transparency is moved through the light path in 1-pixel steps. At each step, the CCD array captures a complete row of image pixels.

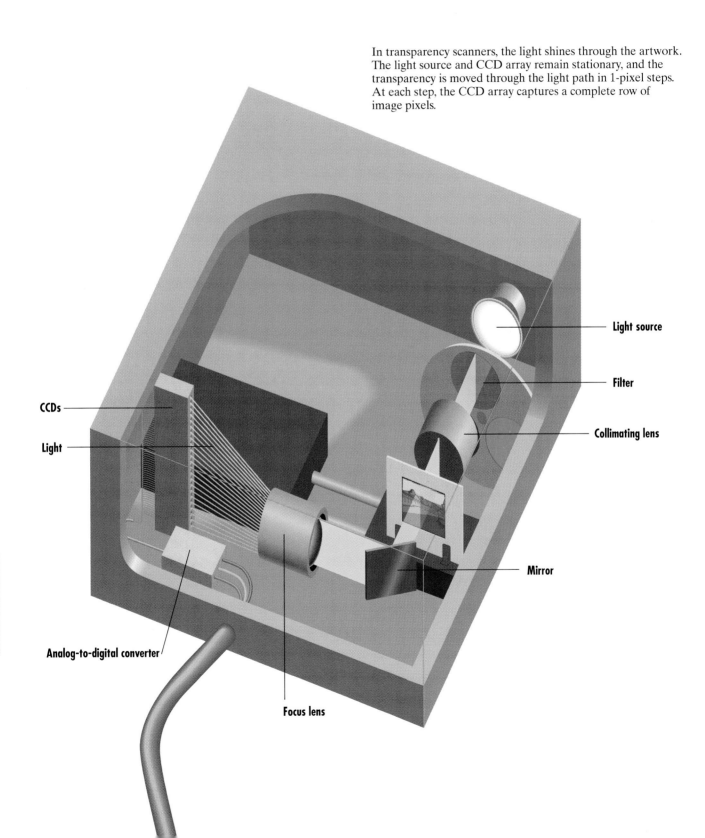

Light source

Filter

Collimating lens

Mirror

CCDs

Light

Analog-to-digital converter

Focus lens

Drum Scanners

Drum scanners produce premium-quality scans, but require considerably more expertise to operate than do flatbed and transparency scanners.

2 During scanning, the drum spins rapidly, exposing each part of the image to the light source and photoreceptors.

1 The artwork to be scanned is mounted on the drum using adhesive tape.

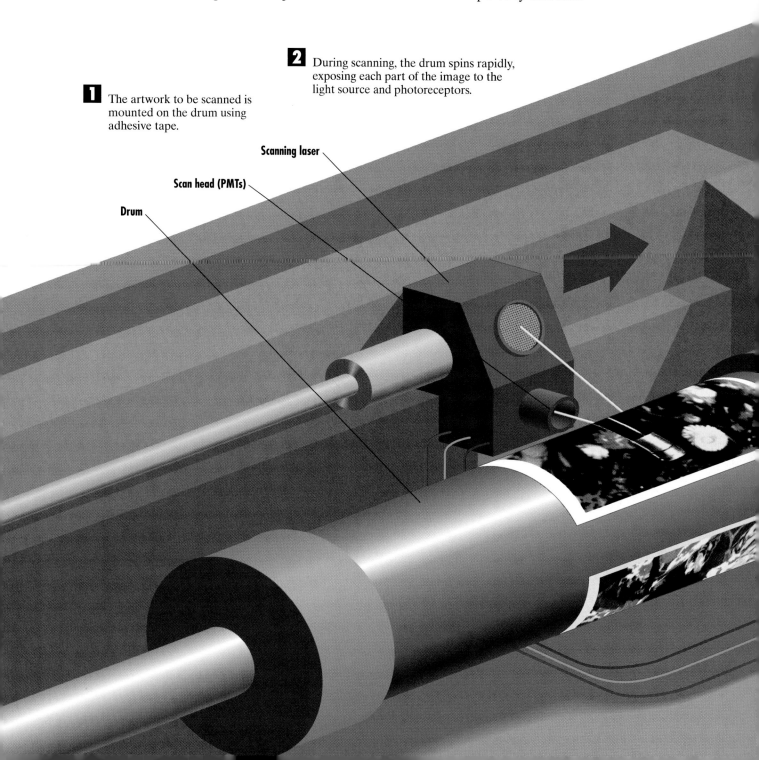

Scanning laser

Scan head (PMTs)

Drum

3 Instead of the CCD arrays used in flatbed and transparency scanners, drum scanners use tube-based photoreceptors called photomultiplier tubes (PMTs). These are more sensitive to low levels of light than are CCDs, so they produce scans that contain better detail in dark areas than do CCD-based scanners. Three PMTs are used, one each for red, green, and blue.

4 The scanning head containing the light source and the PMTs is moved slowly along the length of the drum. The scanner reads a single pixel at a time, rather than the row of pixels captured by a CCD array.

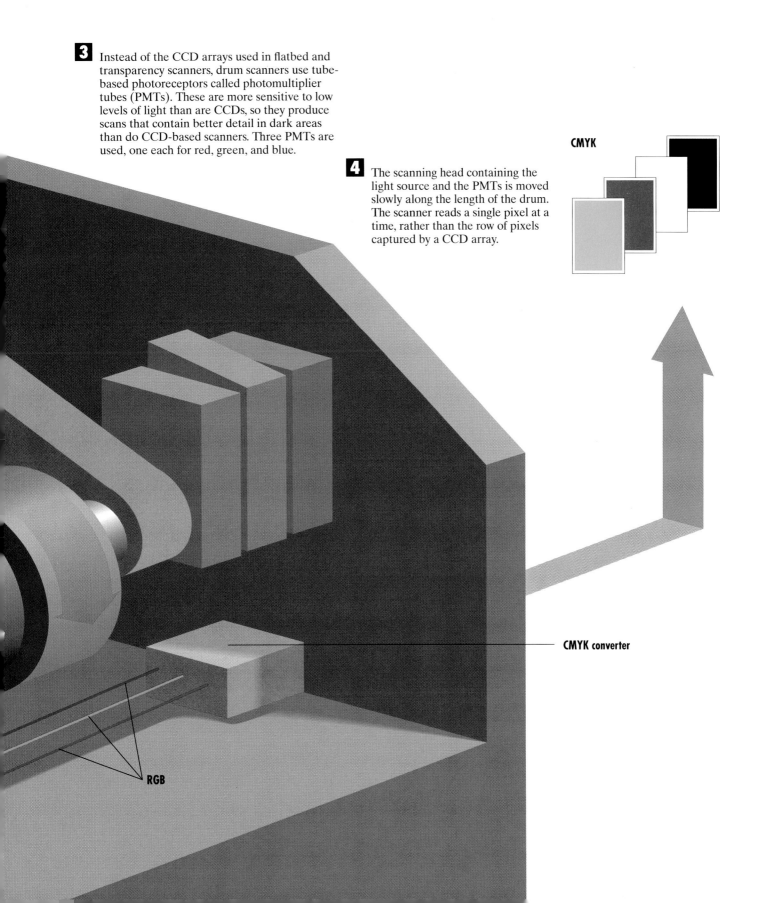

CMYK

CMYK converter

RGB

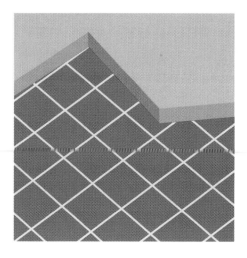

CHAPTER 15

How Graphic Input Devices Work

F YOUR COMPUTER setup includes a mouse and a keyboard, you already use two input devices. But there are other input devices geared toward graphics—in addition to scanners—that are of special interest to desktop publishers.

Graphics tablets consist of two components: a pointing device and the tablet itself. The pointing device is either a *puck*, a precision tracing device that has a sighting hole with plastic crosshairs, or a *stylus*, a pen-like device that runs on batteries or that attaches to the tablet with a cord. The tablet, a thin, rigid pad that connects to the computer, contains a fine grid that maps to pixels on the computer screen. Drawing the pointing device across the tablet makes a corresponding line on your computer screen.

A stylus and graphics tablet can be used as a mouse substitute for pointing and clicking (some people claim the stylus is ergonomically superior to a mouse). But graphics tablets really come into their own with graphics software containing tools designed specifically for the tablet. A puck is used primarily for precision drawings such as technical engineering illustrations and computer-aided design (CAD). A stylus is used for more free-form drawing. Graphics software that supports pressure-sensitive pens and tablets allows you to draw lines of varying widths by changing the pressure or angle of the stylus on the pad, or to add realistic-looking shading to illustrations by sketching on the pad as you would with charcoal or pastel chalks.

We've already seen how scanners are used as input devices to bring in hard-copy photographs and illustrations. New developments in photography and computers are conspiring to eliminate that step. Digital cameras let you take photographs that bypass the film process by directly capturing the image as digital data, which you then load into your system by connecting the camera to the computer. The process takes minutes, compared to days required by the traditional system of processing, printing, and scanning the film before it can be used.

But such cameras are expensive. A consumer-oriented twist on digital photography is being promoted by Eastman Kodak Company, whose Photo CD system lets you drop off your film for processing at your local photofinisher and receive in return a CD-ROM of the images as well as the prints and negatives. You can open these images on your computer and use them in layouts, or view them on your television screen if you have the correct CD-ROM player.

Graphics Tablets

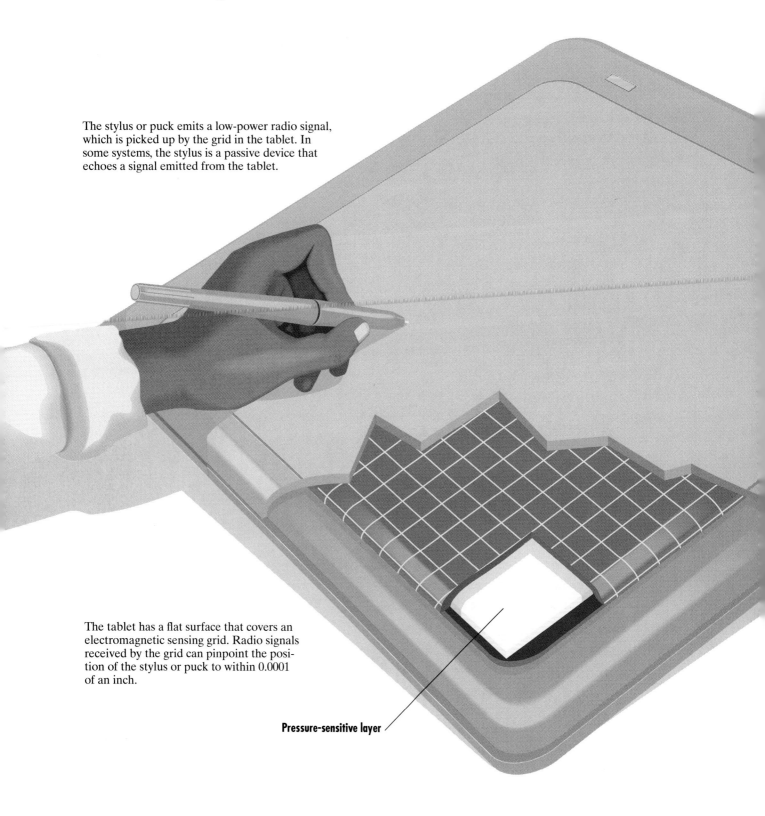

The stylus or puck emits a low-power radio signal, which is picked up by the grid in the tablet. In some systems, the stylus is a passive device that echoes a signal emitted from the tablet.

The tablet has a flat surface that covers an electromagnetic sensing grid. Radio signals received by the grid can pinpoint the position of the stylus or puck to within 0.0001 of an inch.

Pressure-sensitive layer

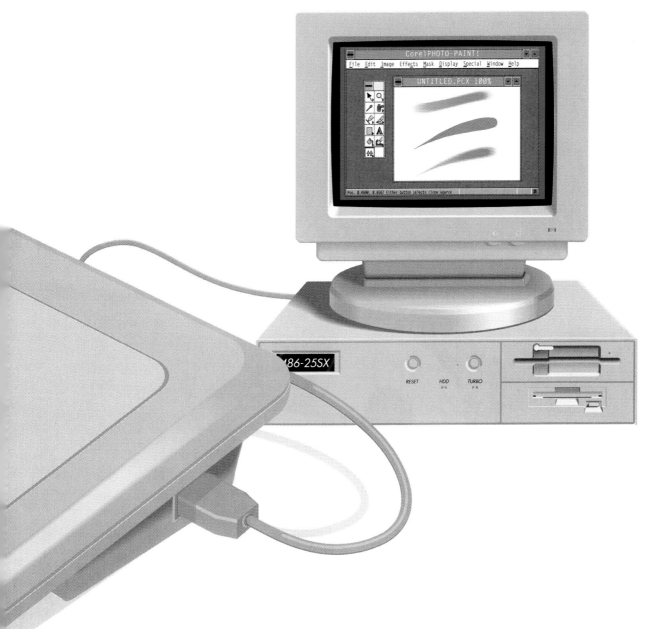

Unlike the mouse, a graphics tablet is an *absolute positioning device*. A given location on the tablet always corresponds to exactly the same point on the screen. In addition to position, some styli can also transmit information about how hard the stylus is being pressed against the tablet. Software that supports pressure-sensitive styli allows the artist to draw or paint in a very natural way, varying the width of the stroke or the density of the electronic paint, with the amount of pressure applied to the stylus.

Digital Cameras

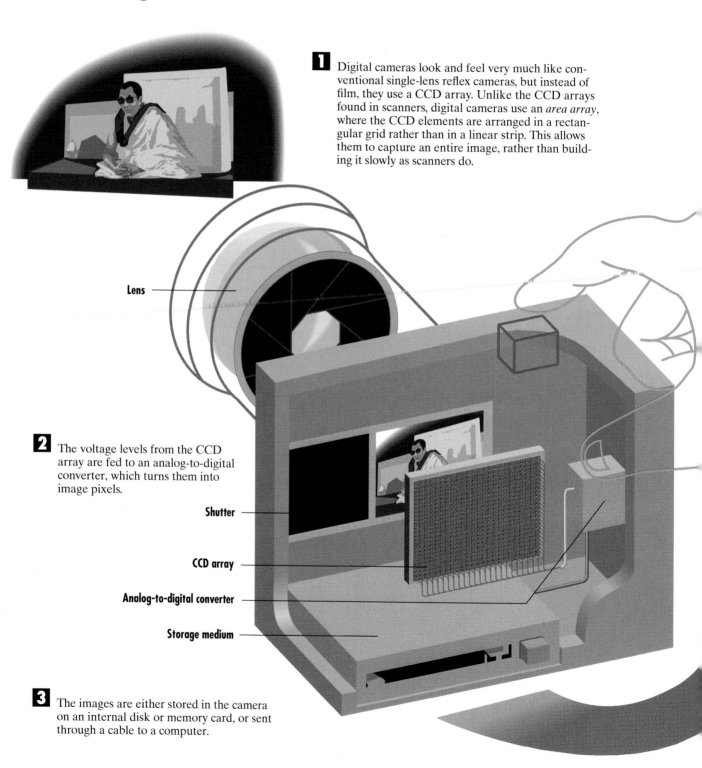

1 Digital cameras look and feel very much like conventional single-lens reflex cameras, but instead of film, they use a CCD array. Unlike the CCD arrays found in scanners, digital cameras use an *area array*, where the CCD elements are arranged in a rectangular grid rather than in a linear strip. This allows them to capture an entire image, rather than building it slowly as scanners do.

Lens

2 The voltage levels from the CCD array are fed to an analog-to-digital converter, which turns them into image pixels.

Shutter

CCD array

Analog-to-digital converter

Storage medium

3 The images are either stored in the camera on an internal disk or memory card, or sent through a cable to a computer.

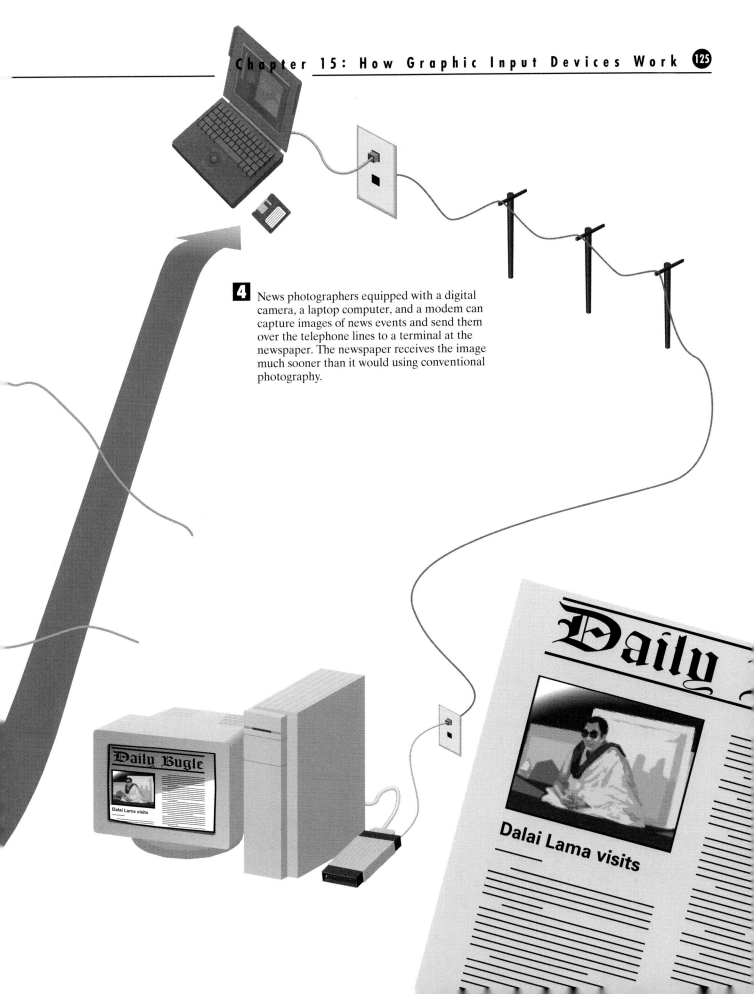

4 News photographers equipped with a digital camera, a laptop computer, and a modem can capture images of news events and send them over the telephone lines to a terminal at the newspaper. The newspaper receives the image much sooner than it would using conventional photography.

Daily Bugle

Dalai Lama visits

Daíly

Dalai Lama visits

Photo CD System

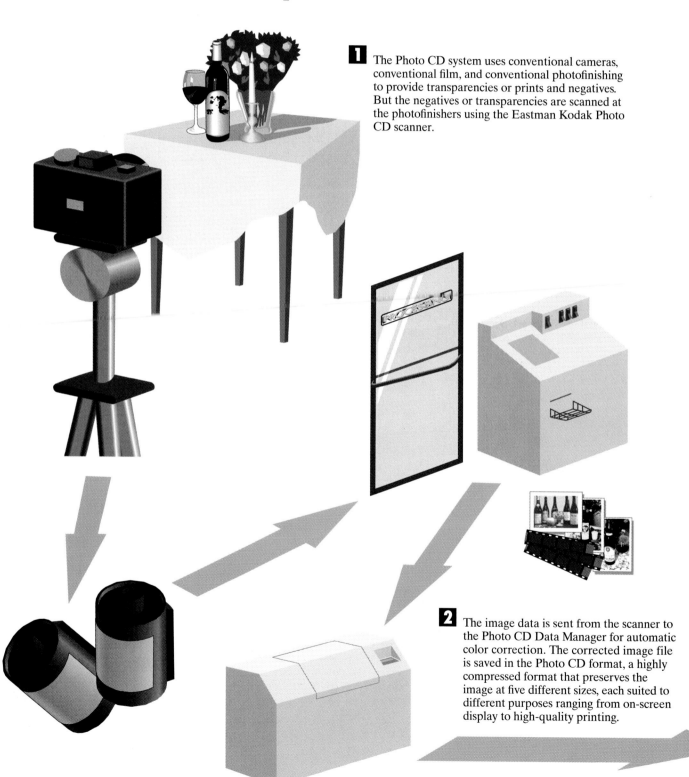

1 The Photo CD system uses conventional cameras, conventional film, and conventional photofinishing to provide transparencies or prints and negatives. But the negatives or transparencies are scanned at the photofinishers using the Eastman Kodak Photo CD scanner.

2 The image data is sent from the scanner to the Photo CD Data Manager for automatic color correction. The corrected image file is saved in the Photo CD format, a highly compressed format that preserves the image at five different sizes, each suited to different purposes ranging from on-screen display to high-quality printing.

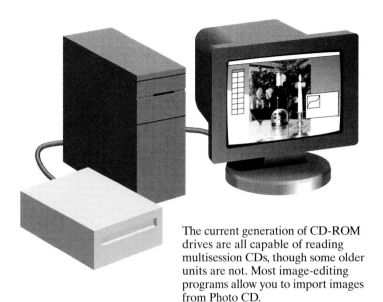

The current generation of CD-ROM drives are all capable of reading multisession CDs, though some older units are not. Most image-editing programs allow you to import images from Photo CD.

You can play Photo CDs on a Photo CD player, which displays Photo CD images on a conventional television set. Some multi-purpose drives plug into stereo systems to play audio CDs, plug into computers to read CD-ROMs (including Photo CDs), and play Photo CDs on television sets.

3 The image files are sent to the Kodak Photo CD Writer, where they're written to a Photo CD. Each CD-ROM can hold about 100 images. Unlike conventional CD-ROMs, you can add data to Photo CDs more than once—a capability called *multisession recording*. This means that you can take the same CD back to the photofinisher and have more images added until the disc is full. Like other CDs, you can't alter the data once it's been written.

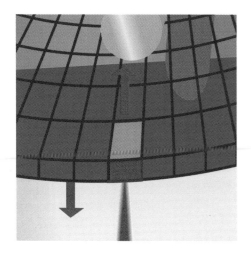

CHAPTER
16

How Storage Devices Work

WHEN IT COMES to hard disks, bigger is always better. Nowhere is this truer than in desktop publishing, where a page layout program requires 20 megabytes to install, font libraries easily inch up to another 40 megabytes, and a single high-resolution color image consumes 50 to 75 megabytes. Then there's the matter of keeping several versions of a project hanging around before the final version is completed, and the problem of archiving your publications for posterity or recycling them into new projects.

Although the price of hard disks continues to decline (to about a dollar a megabyte on average), buying a new hard disk when you've filled up the old one isn't possible for most people. That's why removable media drives are a wise investment for desktop publishers. Removable media consist of storage media encased in a disk, cartridge, or cassette, and a drive capable of reading them. Their capacities vary, but when one cartridge is full, you simply pop in another. This approach gives you endless storage as well as portability. Instead of carting around a hard drive, you can simply take the cartridge with you.

Known by their brand names, SyQuest (made by SyQuest International) and Bernoulli (made by Iomega Corporation) drives are popular with publishers who take their pages to service bureaus. Using read/write heads and magentic media, these devices are much like removable hard disks and, typically, hold between 44 and 150 megabytes of data, although capacities are increasing all the time.

Magneto-optical drives use a technology based on laser beams and plastic media. They can hold well over a gigabyte of information, but they tend to be slow, making them better for archive and backup purposes than for accessing images you use regularly. Digital audio tape (DAT) is, like its musical counterpart, a high-quality medium that's well suited for backing up your system and archiving data. A single DAT can hold up to 8 or more gigabytes of data. But locating a specific file on a DAT can take a relatively long time, so DAT is mostly used for archiving and backup.

CD-ROM stands for *compact disc-read only memory,* which as its name implies, means that you can only write data to a CD-ROM once, after which it can't be changed. CD-ROM can hold up to 600 megabytes of data but cost only pennies to manufacture, so they're used primarily as a distribution medium for software that you can import into a publication or install on your hard disk.

Removable Storage Media

Magneto-optical (MO) drives use a laser beam to change the magnetic polarity of the plastic disk on which the data resides. Although MO drives are expensive, the cartridges themselves are relatively inexpensive, so they offer a cost-effective solution for archiving large amounts of data. However, MO drives are too slow to substitute for a conventional hard disk as primary storage.

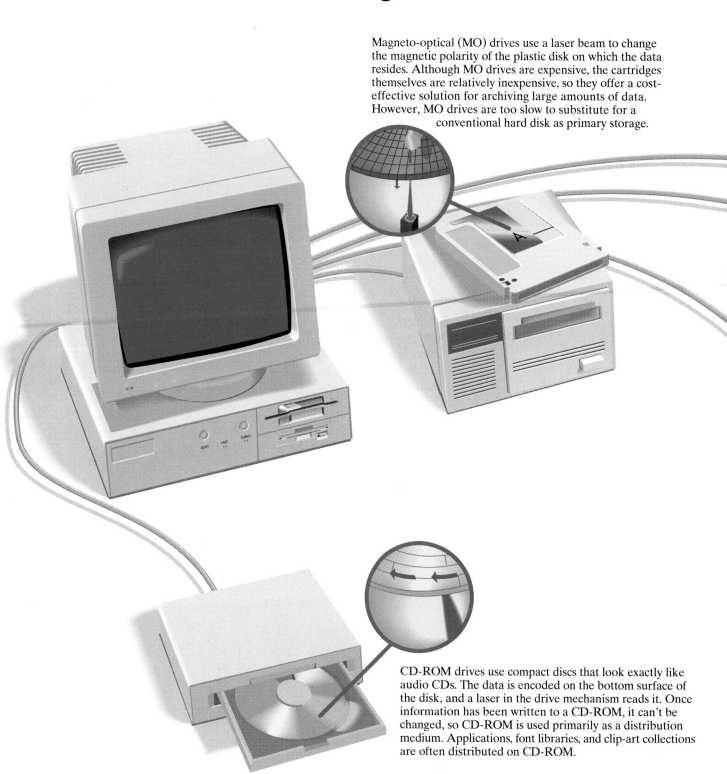

CD-ROM drives use compact discs that look exactly like audio CDs. The data is encoded on the bottom surface of the disk, and a laser in the drive mechanism reads it. Once information has been written to a CD-ROM, it can't be changed, so CD-ROM is used primarily as a distribution medium. Applications, font libraries, and clip-art collections are often distributed on CD-ROM.

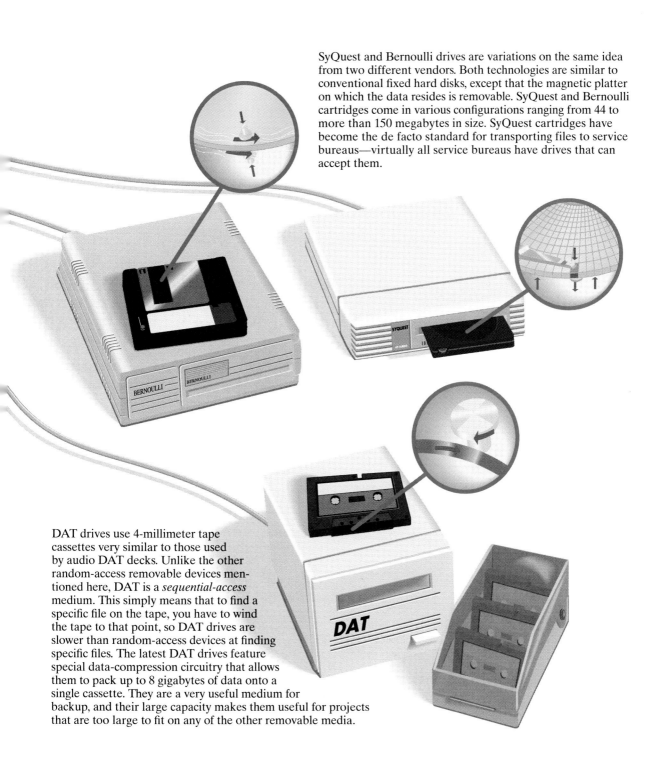

SyQuest and Bernoulli drives are variations on the same idea from two different vendors. Both technologies are similar to conventional fixed hard disks, except that the magnetic platter on which the data resides is removable. SyQuest and Bernoulli cartridges come in various configurations ranging from 44 to more than 150 megabytes in size. SyQuest cartridges have become the de facto standard for transporting files to service bureaus—virtually all service bureaus have drives that can accept them.

DAT drives use 4-millimeter tape cassettes very similar to those used by audio DAT decks. Unlike the other random-access removable devices mentioned here, DAT is a *sequential-access* medium. This simply means that to find a specific file on the tape, you have to wind the tape to that point, so DAT drives are slower than random-access devices at finding specific files. The latest DAT drives feature special data-compression circuitry that allows them to pack up to 8 gigabytes of data onto a single cassette. They are a very useful medium for backup, and their large capacity makes them useful for projects that are too large to fit on any of the other removable media.

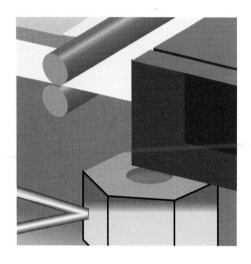

How Printers Work

EVERY DESKTOP PUBLISHING system needs a printer, whether it's used for proofing, for making camera-ready output, or for producing the final printed piece. After all, the printed page is what desktop publishing is all about.

The choice of desktop printers is huge, ranging from modest black-and-white ink-jet printers costing hundreds of dollars, to heavy-duty color laser printers that can form the heart of an on-demand color publishing system, to high-resolution PostScript imagesetters capable of producing negatives for use in high-quality offset printing.

Laser printers are the workhorses of desktop publishing, and they're getting faster and cheaper all the time. Few desktop publishers buy imagesetters or color laser copiers, relying instead on service bureaus for output from those devices. But a PostScript laser printer is invaluable for proofing black-and-white pages destined for service bureau output. If you're using the laser printer to produce either camera-ready copy or the final output itself, PostScript may not be absolutely necessary, but if you rely on service bureaus for final output, it's a good idea to have a PostScript printer.

Publishers buy color printers for two key purposes: as a design aid and as a proofing device. It's important to understand the difference between producing proofs and comps. *Comprehensives*, or *comps*, show the position, orientation, and integration of type and graphics. Designers use comps as a design aid, to assess work in progress, and to show to clients for initial approval. Proofing, in the strictest sense of the word, is a procedure in which the designer or publisher checks a layout to make sure that placement and color are correct and the film for the photographic plates have no flaws.

PostScript laser printers are reliable proofing devices for black-and-white or single-color jobs, but no desktop printer will produce a completely reliable proof for color work. Some color desktop printers attempt to reproduce spot colors, such as those from the popular Pantone color library, but as we described in Chapter 13, it's difficult to match colors accurately throughout the desktop production chain, so desktop color printers are used primarily to produce comps.

Inexpensive ink-jet printers, which use tiny nozzles to precisely spray water-soluble inks on paper, may be used for printing comps. The print quality of ink-jet printers is lower than that of laser printers, and they tend to be very slow, but they provide a low-cost solution for printing color comps.

Thermal-wax printers use colored wax instead of ink. They produce stronger color than cheap ink-jets, and they're much faster, but they're also more expensive—both to purchase and to run.

Dye-sublimation printers use transparent dyes rather than opaque inks, which lets them produce near-photographic continuous-tone output. Some adventurous sites are beginning to use dye-sublimation printers as a substitute for more traditional proofing methods, but they're more often used to make high-quality comps.

PostScript imagesetters use essentially the same technology as laser printers do, but they print at a much higher resolution on photosensitive paper or film, instead of using toner on plain paper. Most jobs that are printed on a press use an imagesetter to produce the camera-ready artwork from which the plates are made.

How Ink-Jet Printers Work

Ink-jet printers offer low-cost color output, some on plain paper. However, they're slow and tend to have a limited range of color, so they're used mostly for rough comps.

1 The printing assembly—the print head and the ink reservoirs—passes from side to side across the paper.

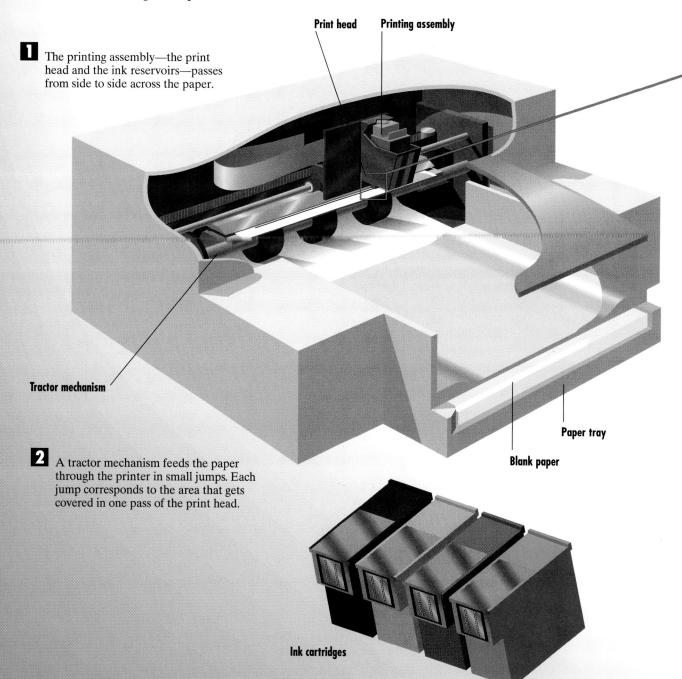

Print head

Printing assembly

Tractor mechanism

Paper tray

Blank paper

2 A tractor mechanism feeds the paper through the printer in small jumps. Each jump corresponds to the area that gets covered in one pass of the print head.

Ink cartridges

Heating element

Nozzle

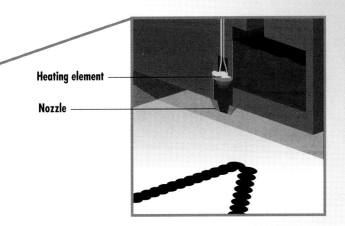

3 The print head contains a heating element that heats the liquid ink to boiling point. When the ink boils, the increased pressure forces it through the nozzles in the print head and onto the page, where it dries. The amount of ink on the page is controlled by varying the temperature of the heating element in the print head.

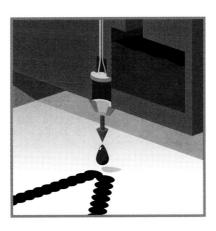

How Laser Printers Work

Laser printers and imagesetters use similar technologies. In both types of devices, a bitmapped image of the page is created by the raster image processor, and is then sent to the laser as a series of pulses. The laser flashes on and off, and as it does so, the beam is reflected across the width of the receiving medium. A row of dots is "painted" on the receiver in laser light: When the laser flashes on, it creates a dot, and when it's off, it leaves a blank spot. Then the receiver is rotated a small amount, and the process is repeated, so the image of the page is built up row by row on the receiving medium.

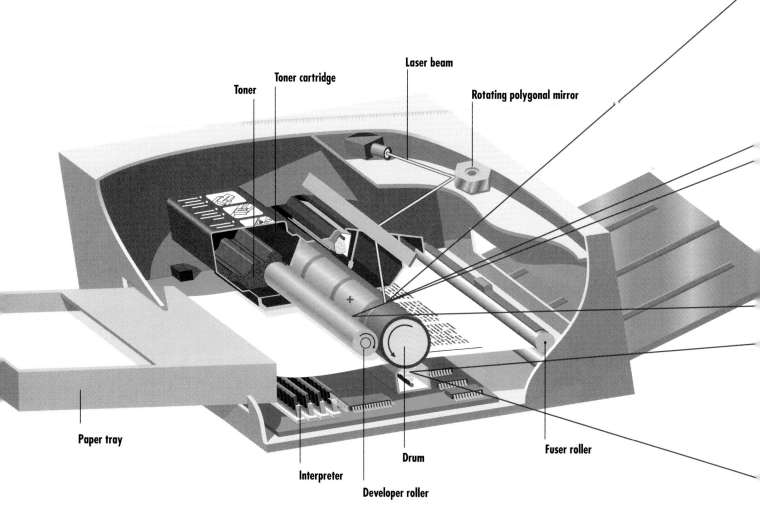

Laser beam

Toner cartridge

Toner

Rotating polygonal mirror

Paper tray

Interpreter

Developer roller

Drum

Fuser roller

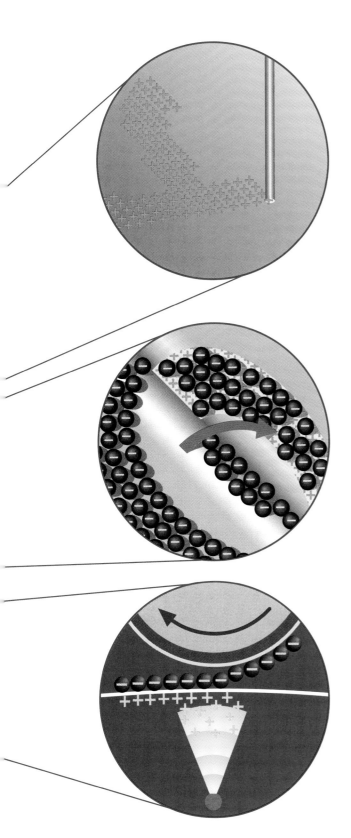

1 In a laser printer, the receiving medium is a photosensitive drum, known either as the OPC (organo-photoconductor) or simply as the drum. The drum holds an electrical charge, and the polarity of the charge changes where the laser beam strikes the drum, so the page image is painted on the drum in a pattern of electrical charge.

2 A developer roller picks up toner from the toner hopper. The toner holds the same charge as the drum, so it is repelled from the drum, except for those areas that have had their polarity changed by the laser beam. These areas attract the toner. As the paper passes through the printer, a charge is applied to it of opposite polarity to the charge of the toner, so the toner is transferred from the drum to the paper, forming the image.

3 Finally, the toner is fused to the paper by passing it through a pair of heated fuser rollers, which melt the toner and make it stick to the paper.

How Imagesetters Work

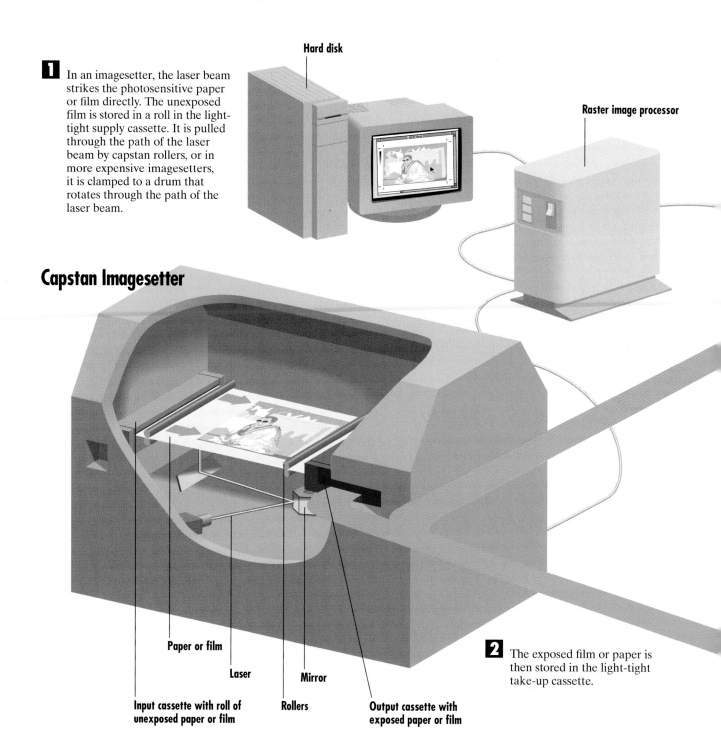

1 In an imagesetter, the laser beam strikes the photosensitive paper or film directly. The unexposed film is stored in a roll in the light-tight supply cassette. It is pulled through the path of the laser beam by capstan rollers, or in more expensive imagesetters, it is clamped to a drum that rotates through the path of the laser beam.

Hard disk

Raster image processor

Capstan Imagesetter

Paper or film

Laser

Mirror

Input cassette with roll of unexposed paper or film

Rollers

Output cassette with exposed paper or film

2 The exposed film or paper is then stored in the light-tight take-up cassette.

Drum Imagesetter

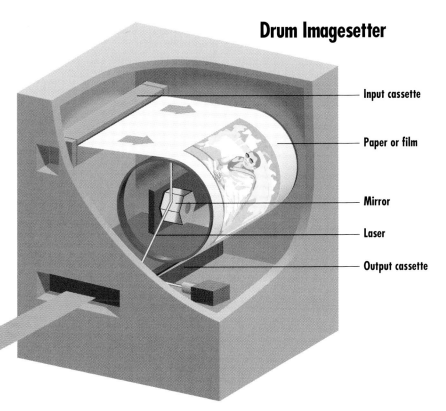

Input cassette

Paper or film

Mirror

Laser

Output cassette

3 The take-up cassette is removed from the imagesetter and fed into the film processor, where the film or paper is developed using conventional photographic techniques. Since the image is created by the laser shining directly on photosensitive material, the resulting image is much sharper than one made up of blobs of toner sticking to paper.

Film Processor

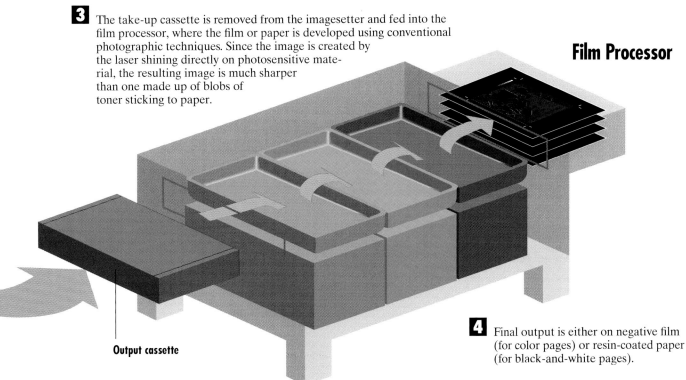

Output cassette

4 Final output is either on negative film (for color pages) or resin-coated paper (for black-and-white pages).

How Color Thermal-Wax-Transfer and Dye-Sublimation Printers Work

Thermal-wax-transfer and dye-sublimation printers work in a very similar fashion, so much so that some hybrid printers are available that can function as both a thermal-wax printer and a dye-sublimation printer, depending on the medium loaded.

Thermal-Wax-Transfer Printer

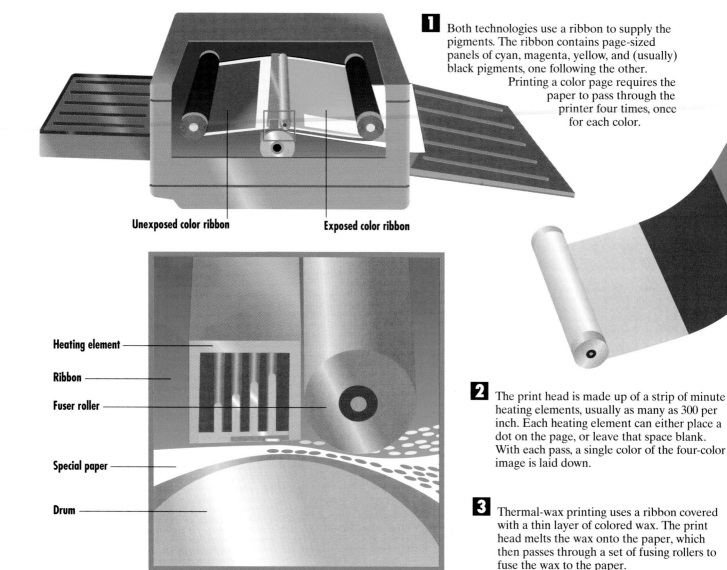

1 Both technologies use a ribbon to supply the pigments. The ribbon contains page-sized panels of cyan, magenta, yellow, and (usually) black pigments, one following the other. Printing a color page requires the paper to pass through the printer four times, once for each color.

Unexposed color ribbon

Exposed color ribbon

Heating element

Ribbon

Fuser roller

Special paper

Drum

2 The print head is made up of a strip of minute heating elements, usually as many as 300 per inch. Each heating element can either place a dot on the page, or leave that space blank. With each pass, a single color of the four-color image is laid down.

3 Thermal-wax printing uses a ribbon covered with a thin layer of colored wax. The print head melts the wax onto the paper, which then passes through a set of fusing rollers to fuse the wax to the paper.

Dye-Sublimation Printer

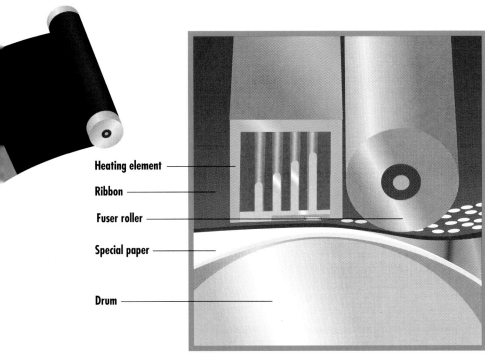

Heating element

Ribbon

Fuser roller

Special paper

Drum

4 Dye-sublimation ribbons contain translucent dyes instead of wax. The print head vaporizes the dye, which then condenses in the coating of the special paper.

5 By varying the temperature of the print head, the precise amount of each dye laid down for each dot can be carefully controlled. Unlike other color printing technologies, where dots of the different colors are placed adjacent to one another, dye-sublimation printers print the different colors directly on top of each other, with no gaps between the dots. Variations in color are reproduced by varying the amount of each dye laid down, rather than by changing the size of the dot.

PREPRESS

CONTENTS

Chapter 18: How Printing Presses Work
148

Chapter 19: How Color Separations Work
152

Chapter 20: How Trapping Works
158

Chapter 21: How Imposition Works
162

Chapter 22: How Proofing Works
166

UNLESS YOUR PUBLICATION is destined to be produced in small numbers on a photocopy machine, your final pages will almost certainly be produced on a printing press. Desktop publishers quickly find that there's a world of difference between the pure mathematical entities of electronic pages and the very physical process of putting ink on paper at high speeds. To print electronic pages correctly and economically on the press, several tasks must be undertaken to prepare the electronic pages for press output.

Prepress is the term used to describe all the tasks that go into converting camera-ready artwork into plates that can be used on the printing press. Traditionally, this has covered everything from color separation and halftone production to platemaking and everything in between, such as trapping to correct for misregistration on the press, and imposition, where pages are assembled into large sheets of paper called signatures.

But desktop technology has had its impact on the prepress process, too, to the point where there are now many businesses that describe themselves as electronic prepress shops. As a desktop publisher, you may prefer to leave some or all of the prepress tasks to a service bureau or a prepress house, but you should still have some idea of what they do. After all, you pay for their services, and a familiarity with the prepress process can help you to avoid creating designs that are beautiful but almost impossible to reproduce.

To understand why prepress houses do the things they do, it helps if you understand the basic mechanics of printing, and what happens when ink hits paper on the press. A great deal of prepress work consists of building elements into the electronic page that will compensate for the press irregularities resulting from ink hitting quickly moving paper, so in Chapter 18, we look at printing presses, and how they work.

The halftone process is vital to printing, but digital output devices such as image-setters and laser printers can't print true variable-sized dots, so they have to simulate them. The resolution of the output device imposes limitations on the halftones that can be produced—until you get to high resolutions, you must make a trade-off between the amount of fine detail in the image and the number of shades of gray it contains. In Chapter 19, we first examine the digital halftone process. Then, we look at the art and science of creating color separations.

For color work, color separations must be made. The press can only lay down a single color of ink at a time, so a separate plate must be made for each color of ink used. When the design calls for screened tints, or when the four-color process is used to reproduce a wide range of color, the separations must also be made into halftones, and the halftones must be set at different angles. The choice of angles is critical, as an error in the screen angles will produce unwanted moiré patterns on the final printed page.

In color work, where each ink is laid down separately, *registration*, the alignment of the paper on the press, becomes a critical issue. Few if any presses are capable of maintaining perfect registration throughout a print run, so trapping is applied to the electronic files to prevent gaps between abutting colors when the press fails to register them correctly. In Chapter 20, we look at how trapping works.

Desktop publishers typically think in terms of single pages, but commercial printers rarely print a single page at a time. Instead, pages are grouped into *signatures*, large sheets of 4, 8, 16, or 32 pages, which are then folded and cut to make the final publication. The process of grouping the pages together into a signature is called imposition, and again, it's necessary to build in to the electronic prepress process some factors that compensate for the irregularities of the press. In Chapter 21, we look at the process of imposition.

Press runs are expensive, so it's vital to ensure that your electronic pages are correctly set up for the press before you start the press run. To do this, proofs are made throughout the production process. The final proof, or *contract proof*, serves as the basis of the understanding between client and printer as to the appearance of the final pages. In Chapter 22, we examine the proofing process, and look at various types of proofing methods and their strengths and weaknesses

How Printing Presses Work

I F YOUR PUBLICATION requires more than 800 or so copies, it's almost certainly cheaper to print it on a printing press than it is to reproduce it by photocopying or other means. Printing presses must be prepared for a print job—the process of mounting the plate on the press and setting the ink and water mixture correctly is known as *makeready*—so the press isn't economical for very short runs, although the break-even point is changing as presses become more automated.

The most common printing process is known as offset lithography. It is based on the fact that grease and water don't mix. When printing plates are made, the parts of the plate that contain the image are treated to receive grease and repel water, while the blank areas are made to receive water and repel grease. When the plate is mounted on the press, it comes into contact first with the dampening roller, which wets the blank areas with water or a dampening solution. Then it comes into contact with the ink roller, which wets the printing areas with ink—the blank areas repel the ink.

The image is then *offset,* or transferred from the plate to the *blanket cylinder,* which has a soft rubber surface. The paper passes between the blanket cylinder and the *impression cylinder,* and the image is transferred from the blanket cylinder to the paper. Offset lithography presses may be sheetfed or web presses. Sheetfed offset lithography presses, which accept large sheets of paper, are commonly used for posters, labels, packaging, and fine-art reproduction. Web presses, which accept huge rolls of paper, are generally used for high-volume, long-run jobs such as newspapers, books, and magazines.

A less common printing technique called gravure is an example of *intaglio printing*, which uses a sunken or depressed surface for the image. The image area is made up of wells etched into a copper cylinder or wraparound plate, which rotates in a bath of ink. The depressed areas pick up the ink, and excess ink is wiped off the surface of the plate by a flexible steel blade called the doctor blade. The ink remaining in the cells is transferred directly to the paper as it passes between the plate cylinder and the impression cylinder. A distinguishing feature of gravure is that the entire image, including type and line art, is screened. As with offset lithography, gravure presses may be sheetfed or web, the latter process is known as *rotogravure*. Rotogravure is commonly used for Sunday newspaper magazine sections, newspaper color, wallpaper, and large mail-order catalogs.

Printing Processes

While one- and two-color presses are still in common use, modern printing presses are set up, typically, to handle four or more ink colors. In the scenario shown here, the press consists of five printing mechanisms—one for each of the four process colors cyan, magenta, yellow, and black, and one for a premixed spot color ink. The paper moves through a succession of cylinders that each transfer the appropriate ink to the paper in controlled amounts on specific areas.

Offset Lithography

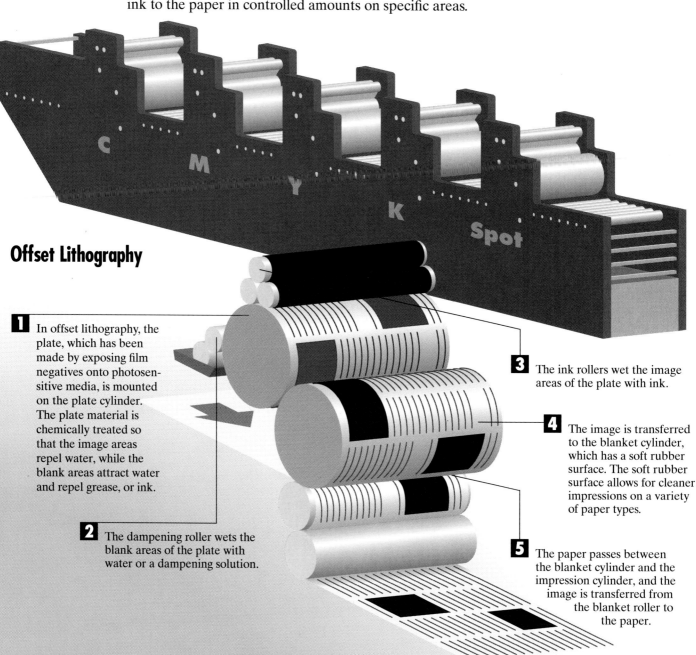

1 In offset lithography, the plate, which has been made by exposing film negatives onto photosensitive media, is mounted on the plate cylinder. The plate material is chemically treated so that the image areas repel water, while the blank areas attract water and repel grease, or ink.

2 The dampening roller wets the blank areas of the plate with water or a dampening solution.

3 The ink rollers wet the image areas of the plate with ink.

4 The image is transferred to the blanket cylinder, which has a soft rubber surface. The soft rubber surface allows for cleaner impressions on a variety of paper types.

5 The paper passes between the blanket cylinder and the impression cylinder, and the image is transferred from the blanket roller to the paper.

Gravure

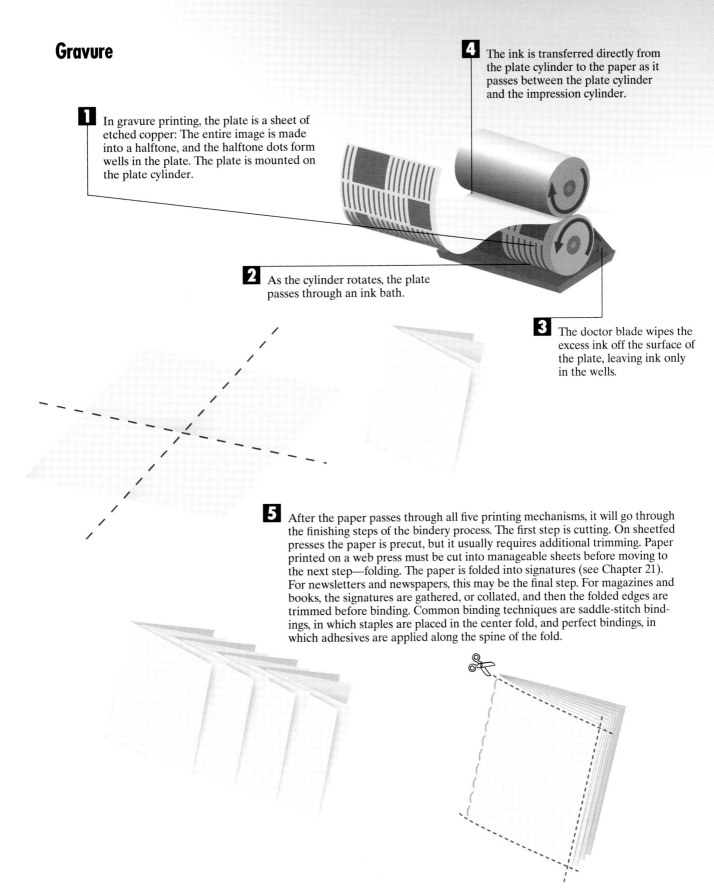

1 In gravure printing, the plate is a sheet of etched copper: The entire image is made into a halftone, and the halftone dots form wells in the plate. The plate is mounted on the plate cylinder.

4 The ink is transferred directly from the plate cylinder to the paper as it passes between the plate cylinder and the impression cylinder.

2 As the cylinder rotates, the plate passes through an ink bath.

3 The doctor blade wipes the excess ink off the surface of the plate, leaving ink only in the wells.

5 After the paper passes through all five printing mechanisms, it will go through the finishing steps of the bindery process. The first step is cutting. On sheetfed presses the paper is precut, but it usually requires additional trimming. Paper printed on a web press must be cut into manageable sheets before moving to the next step—folding. The paper is folded into signatures (see Chapter 21). For newsletters and newspapers, this may be the final step. For magazines and books, the signatures are gathered, or collated, and then the folded edges are trimmed before binding. Common binding techniques are saddle-stitch bindings, in which staples are placed in the center fold, and perfect bindings, in which adhesives are applied along the spine of the fold.

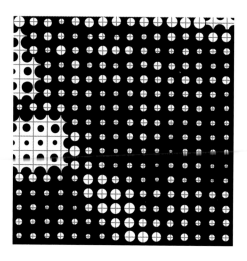

CHAPTER 19

How Color Separations Work

PHOTOGRAPHIC IMAGES, like real life, contain millions of colors, but printing presses see everything in black and white, or rather, ink and paper. Color is introduced only by the ink. It's impractical to use millions of different inks, so print reproduces color by combining varying amounts of cyan, magenta, yellow, and black inks, laid down in overlapping halftone patterns.

Halftones work because the human eye can't distinguish two points when they're separated by only one minute of arc—equivalent to $\frac{1}{250}$ of an inch at a reading distance of 12 inches. So the eye can be fooled into perceiving different shades by a pattern of small equally spaced dots of varying sizes, as long as the dots are placed close together.

Let's start with the simplest example, reproducing a photograph on a printing press using black ink and white paper. If you examine a newspaper photograph closely, you'll see that it's made up of a pattern of dots. The dots are large in the dark areas of the image, intermediate-sized in the middle grays, and very small in the bright areas, but the distance between the centers of the dots is constant. Each dot is printed with the same density and color of ink, but the eye sees shades of gray. The distance between the centers of the dots is determined by the screen applied to the image and is measured as the screen frequency. In the United States the screen frequency is usually expressed in lines per inch (lpi). Typical screen frequencies are 65 to 85 lines per inch for newspapers, 120 to 150 lines per inch for magazines, and 175 lines per inch and up for high-quality art books.

The other factor to consider with a halftone screen is the screen angle. The underlying pattern of dots in a halftone is much more obvious when the screen is oriented at 90 degrees, so in monochrome printing, the screen is usually rotated to 45 degrees. But when you have four colors, you can't simply print the colors one atop the other, because the inks would run into one another and produce a color that looks like mud. Instead, the four halftone screens are rotated to different angles, but this raises another problem. When two screens are superimposed at an angle, it causes an interference pattern called a moiré; the smaller the angle between the screens, the more obvious the moiré. The screen angles used in four-color process printing are a carefully crafted compromise that minimizes moiré.

What Are Halftones?

A *halftone* is a grid of variable-size dots that fools the eye into perceiving continuous gradations of color. Traditionally, halftones—or halftone screens—are the result of photographing an image through a fine mesh screen. In digital publishing systems, the desktop publisher sets the halftone screen in the page layout or graphics program. The appropriate settings appear on the film negatives produced by the imagesetter.

The size of the dots varies according to the shade of gray they simulate, but the centers of the dots are equidistant. The distance between the centers of the dots is called the *screen frequency*, or *screen ruling*. Measured in lines per inch, the higher the screen frequency, the finer the printing possible.

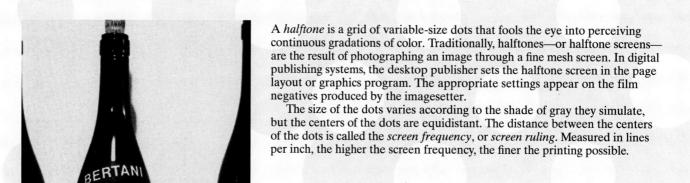

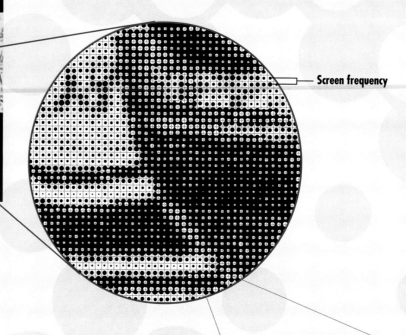

Screen frequency

Digital output devices can't print variable-sized dots. They have a fixed grid of dots, each of which can be printed or left blank, but they're all the same size. Digital printers and imagesetters simulate halftone dots by subdividing their grid of dots into halftone cells. Turning printer dots on and off within the halftone cell changes the size of the halftone dot.

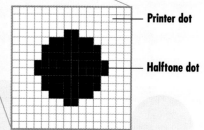

Printer dot

Halftone dot

Halftone cell

2400 dpi, 133 lpi

The number of dots in the halftone cell is equal to the printer's resolution divided by the screen frequency, and it dictates the number of shades of gray the device can produce at a given screen frequency. Good image reproduction requires about 256 shades of gray, which can be achieved with a 2400-dpi imagesetter using a 150-line screen, resulting in a 16-by-16-dot halftone cell.

With a lower-resolution device, you must trade off gray levels for screen frequency. A lower screen frequency means a halftone cell with more dots, and hence more shades of gray, but the coarseness of the screen makes the halftone dots obvious. A higher screen frequency produces a sharper image, but with fewer shades of gray.

300 dpi, 133 lpi

266 ppi

The resolution of a scanned image has no direct relationship to printer resolution or screen frequency—you can print a scan of any resolution on any printer at any screen frequency, but the quality will be poor unless you have a high enough resolution in both the scanned image and the output device. Images should generally be scanned at twice the frequency of the screen: To print an image at 133 lines per inch, you'd usually scan it at 266 pixels per inch. To reproduce the full tonal range of the image, your output device would need a resolution of at least 2400 dpi.

72 ppi

What Are Process Color Screens and Moirés?

When more than one color ink is used, halftones must be set at different angles so that inks do not print on top of each other. The orientation of one halftone to another is called its screen angle. In traditional printing, the halftone screens were simply set at different angles to each other, then photographed. In digital publishing systems, the imagesetter applies the screen angle, or more adventurous desktop publishers override these default settings and determine their own.

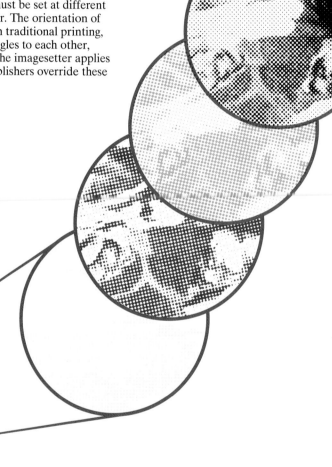

4° offset

18° offset

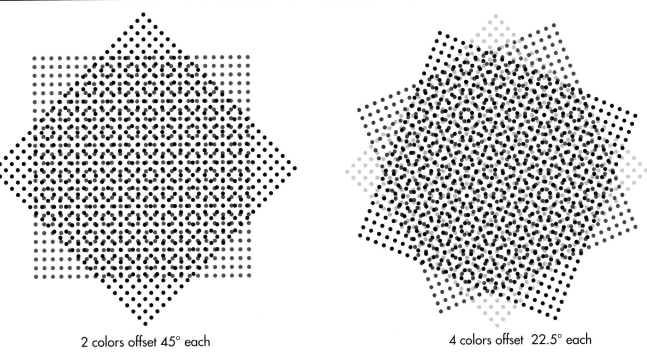

2 colors offset 45° each

4 colors offset 22.5° each

Moiré is the name given to the interference pattern that results when you superimpose two screens at an angle. The smaller the angle, the more obvious the moiré. With two screens, the greatest possible separation is 45 degrees, but in process color, we have to deal with four screens. The greatest possible separation for four screens is 22.5 degrees, which produces a strong moiré pattern, so process color uses a carefully crafted compromise.

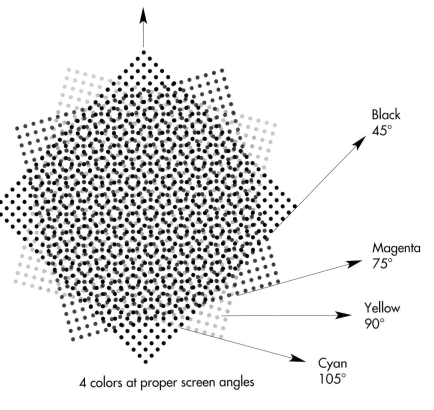

Black
45°

Magenta
75°

Yellow
90°

Cyan
105°

4 colors at proper screen angles

Black is the most obvious color, so the black screen is set at a 45-degree angle, which is the least obvious to the eye.

Cyan and magenta are the next strongest colors, so they are set 30 degrees away from the black screen. Usually, cyan is set at 15 degrees and magenta is set at 75 degrees. Thus, the black, cyan, and magenta screens are set 30 degrees apart from each other—the maximum separation possible for three colors.

This leaves yellow, the least obvious color. If we set it 30 degrees away from any of the other colors, it would overlap one of them, so instead it is set at 90 degrees. This allows 45 degrees of separation from the strongest color, black, and 15 degrees of separation from cyan and magenta. The result is a tight rosette pattern of cyan, magneta, yellow, and black dots.

How Trapping Works

WHEN YOU STOP to consider the sheer mechanical complexity of the average press, the wonder is not that it doesn't work perfectly, but rather that it works as well as it does. But even if the press maintains perfect registration at all times, the paper itself is subject to stretching, so trapping is necessary when two colors abut on the page.

When you use spot colors, you normally set them to *knock out* any color that lies behind them. For example, if you had a blue circle on a yellow background, setting the blue circle to knock out would create a circular white hole in the yellow plate. If you had set the blue circle to *overprint* instead, the yellow plate wouldn't have a hole in it, but the blue circle would come out green, because the yellow background would show through the blue.

However, if the paper stretched or shifted slightly on the press, the blue circle might not print exactly on top of the hole in the yellow plate, and as a result you'd see a white gap between the circle and the background. Trapping is the technique used to address this problem.

Trapping creates a bridge between two colors, filling in any gaps that occur due to misregistration. When two colors meet on the page, the darker color defines the edge of the lighter object, so two kinds of traps are commonly used. A *spread* is used to trap a light object to a dark background; a *choke* is used to trap a dark object to a light background. In both cases, the trap is created using the lighter color; the darker color, which visually defines the edge of the object, is left unchanged.

With process color work, trapping is less of a problem: It's only necessary when two colors that don't share a common component abut. In that case, the usual solution is to create a thin line of an intermediate color. If there's any misregistration, the gap will be filled with one of the process colors rather than white, and as a result, it's much less noticeable.

Some page layout and illustration programs offer limited trapping features, but unless you know what you're doing, it's often a better idea to leave the trapping to the prepress house. You can also design your work so that it doesn't require complex traps.

Trapping

The need for trapping is an inevitable consequence of the printing process. Paper is an elastic substance, and as it passes through the series of rollers on the printing press, it stretches slightly. Printing presses are also slightly imprecise, allowing the paper to shift slightly on the press. The combination of shifting paper and a moving press leads to misregistration of the different colors, resulting in unsightly slivers of blank paper between two adjacent colors. Trapping compensates for these anticipated errors.

C: 0%
M: 80%
Y: 60%
K: 0%

C: 80%
M: 0%
Y: 0%
K: 30%

C: 40%
M: 80%
Y: 20%
K: 0%

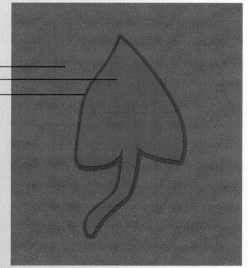

Trapping is easier with process colors because you can mix percentages of colors. If two abutting process colors share a common component, no trapping is necessary, because the common component acts as a bridge between the two colors. When two process colors don't share a common component, you trap them by placing a fine line along the join, made of a color that contains components of both abutting colors.

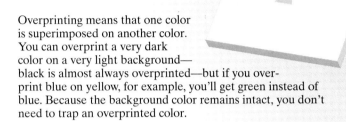

Overprinting means that one color is superimposed on another color. You can overprint a very dark color on a very light background—black is almost always overprinted—but if you overprint blue on yellow, for example, you'll get green instead of blue. Because the background color remains intact, you don't need to trap an overprinted color.

Since overprinting usually gives unpredictable color results, spot colors are usually set to knock out other colors that lie behind them. Knocking out means that a blank space is left behind a colored object. Trapping is almost always required when colors are knocked out, since any misregistration reveals an unsightly sliver of blank paper.

Trapping consists of two techniques—choking and spreading—both of which use selective overprinting. The edge where two colors meet is always defined by the darker color, so you use chokes to trap a dark object to a light background, and spreads to trap a light object to a dark background.

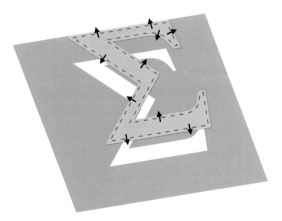

Spreading extends the lighter color object on top of the darker color background.

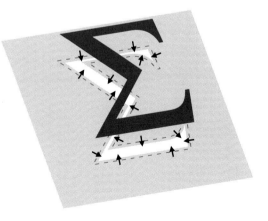

Choking extends a lighter color background behind the darker color object.

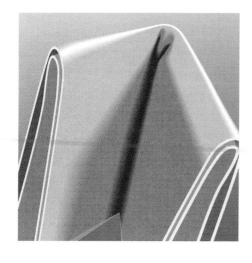

CHAPTER
21

How Imposition Works

GENERALLY, desktop printers print one page at a time, but printing presses print an entire set of pages on a single large sheet, to make the most efficient use of the paper and to provide the highest print speed. This large sheet is called a signature. Depending on the size of the page and the size of the paper, signatures may contain anywhere from 4 to 32 pages.

The process of arranging single pages into a signature, known as imposition, was traditionally the last step before platemaking. It was done manually, by stripping the negatives for each page onto a large sheet called a signature form. Nowadays it may be done electronically, using special imposition software and large-format imagesetters. This combination allows the operator to arrange pages from a page layout program in an electronic signature that prints on a single piece of film.

The pages are arranged so that they appear in the correct order once the signature has been printed, folded, and trimmed. The exact page order depends on the number of pages on the signature and whether the signatures will be nested one inside the other, or stacked one on top of the other. Generally, magazines and newspapers use nested signatures and books use stacked signatures.

In addition to placing the pages in the correct position and order, imposition has to compensate for the behavior of the paper when it's folded. Two principal adjustments involve slightly moving the page image on the signature. *Bottling* compensates for the skewing of the pages as they're folded as a result of large signatures or very thick paper stock. *Shingling* compensates for the way pages in a folded signature tend to move toward the outside edge of the book. The amount of shingling needed increases steadily as you move toward the center signatures of the book.

Once the signature has been printed on both sides, it's cut and folded. The folded signature is then either nested with the others, as in newspapers or magazines, or stacked on top of the others, as in most hardbound books. If you look at a hardbound book, you'll see that the pages are arranged in bundles. Each of these bundles is formed by folding and cutting a single signature.

Nested signatures are either left loose, as in newspapers, or stapled or saddle-stitched, as in many magazines. Stacked signatures are usually stitched individually into the spine of the book. In *perfect binding*, the signatures are collated, ground off at the spine of the book, and then bound with glue so that each page is individually glued to the spine. Whether stacked or nested signatures are used, the final step is to trim the three outside edges of the page.

Imposition

Imposition is the process of arranging individual pages on a large sheet called a signature. In these examples, the sheet of paper will be flipped over and fed back through the press so that both sides of the paper are printed in the correct order. When the signature is cut and folded, the pages are ordered correctly.

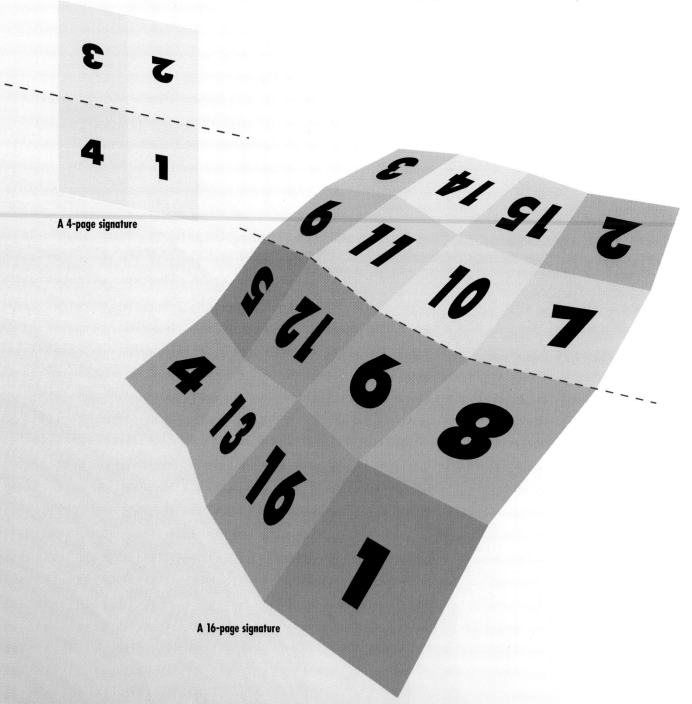

A 4-page signature

A 16-page signature

Bottling compensates for the fact that pages skew when the signature is folded because of the thickness of the paper. The page image is slightly skewed in the opposite direction to counteract the shift. It's particularly important with large signatures and with heavy paper stock.

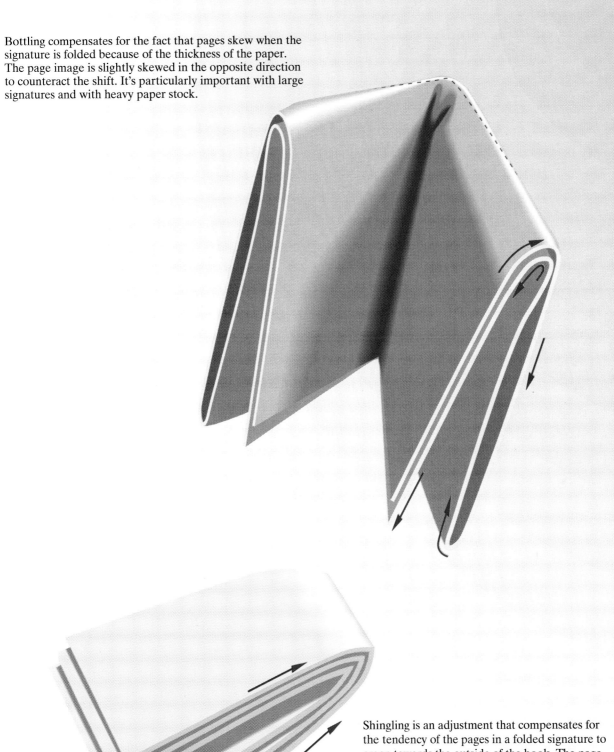

Shingling is an adjustment that compensates for the tendency of the pages in a folded signature to creep towards the outside of the book. The page images are spread further apart to leave room for the fold. The amount of shingling needed is greatest in the center signatures of the book, and least in those nearest the covers.

How Proofing Works

AS WE'VE SEEN in preceding chapters, prepress techniques compensate in advance for problems that may arise during the printing process. But how can you make sure that your colors are accurate, or that your screen angles minimize moirés, or that your trapping settings are correct before you spend the money for a press run? That's where proofing comes in.

A proof lets you check different variables before printing. Usually provided by the print shop or service bureau, a proof serves two important functions: as a guideline for production, and as a contract between the client and the printer. In essence, a proof indicates what you expect as final product.

Because the press introduces its own variables, the most reliable proofs are those obtained close to the end of the production process. *Press proofs* are run off the printing press prior to the final press run. These are the most accurate and most costly proofs and are necessary for fine art books in which exact color and detail are critical.

Composite proofs aren't as accurate as press proofs, but they're the most common proofing method used today because they're relatively cost-effective, and—as they are made from the actual films that will later be used to burn the printing plates—they let you see the halftone dots, screen angles, and frequencies, as well as flaws inherent in the film.

Composite proofs are made by exposing the film negatives onto four sheets of photosensitive media that use the same colors as the printing inks. The four sheets are then either taped together in register to a stiff backing—an *overlay proof*—or placed in register and laminated—an *integral proof* (integral proofs are also referred to by their brand names: MatchPrint by 3M Corp., Chromalin by DuPont, and others). Overlays are less expensive than integrals, but their colors are not as accurate and their registration may be off if the film is not aligned exactly.

With the rise of desktop publishing, digital proofing is gaining popularity. Digital proofing devices, which range from desktop color printers to high-end direct digital color proofing (DDCP) units, vary in price and precision. These devices do not produce proofs from the actual film; therefore, you cannot see what halftones will look like. Many publishers and print-shop personnel reject digital proofs for this reason alone.

As we explained in Chapter 17, desktop color printers are more design tools than proofing devices. Nevertheless, as the color accuracy of these printers improves and their prices decline, some desktop publishers are using dye-sublimation printers as preliminary proofing devices. High-end ink-jet printers are a step above desktop devices, offering improved color fidelity and higher resolutions. They can print on a wide range of paper stocks, allowing you to use the same stock for the proof as will be used for the print job. Finally, DDCP devices attempt to fill the gap between color printers and integral proofs. Like color printers, they accept digital files; and like integral proofers, they produce a laminated, registered page. They also contain software that simulates halftone dots, screen angles, and line frequencies that you'll expect in the final product.

Another area that's piquing interest is *soft proofing*, which bypasses printing altogether by allowing you to view a faithful representation of your pages on a monitor. You can't see any problems that arise from film developing or from the printing process, but you can detect color errors. Standard monitors aren't up to this task, but expensive color-adjusted monitors have been developed for that purpose. At this point they can't replace hard-copy proofs, but as ecological concerns mount, proofing on screen rather than on printed media is provoking interest.

How Proofing Devices Work

Soft proofing allows you to view your pages on screen—you can see gross color and typographic errors before you print out the page. We've noted that different peripherals see color differently, so you cannot rely on a standard monitor as a proofing device. Expensive proprietary workstations offer soft proofing options, and now some monitor manufacturers are developing color-adjusted monitors that will allow you to accurately preview colors on screen. Since ambient lighting dramatically affects how colors are perceived, monitors used for soft proofing come equipped with a light hood and must be kept in a carefully controlled environment.

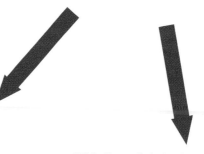

With direct digital color proofing (DDCP) systems, electronic data is transferred to a high-end workstation. The files are then printed on the paper of your choice and laminated as with an integral proof. Although DDCP systems let you skip the step of developing film, the proof contains simulated halftone dots, screen frequencies, and screen angles, allowing you to get a reasonable idea of what your printed page will look like.

Digital proofing device

Soft proofing device

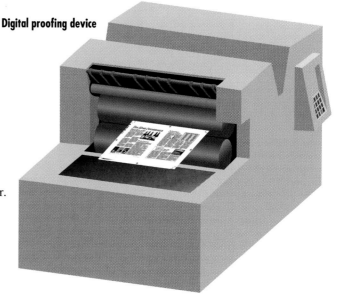

In addition to desktop color printers, a common digital proofing device is a high-end ink-jet printer. With higher resolution and more sophisticated color management than its desktop cousin, an ink-jet printer allows you to print your proof on a variety of paper stocks. As a result, you can print your proof on the exact paper on which your finished piece will be printed.

Negatives

Plate

Press

Next to press proofs, composites are the most accurate proofs used today.

Overlay proof

Overlay proofs consist of layered, transparent sheets carrying pigments corresponding to the ink colors. The sheets are placed in register and taped to a stiff backing.

Another type of composite proof is an *integral proof,* in which the transparent layers are laminated together in register.

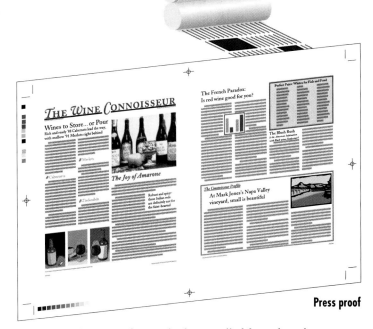

Press proof

Press proofs, sample sheets pulled from the printing press prior to the final press run, are accurate but expensive, since the operator has to set up the press. To correct errors other than those caused by the printing process itself is extremely expensive, so it's a good idea to use other proofing methods to detect problems early on.

THE FUTURE

CONTENTS

Chapter 23: Future Directions
176

Chapter 24: How We Produced This Book
184

THE TREND SINCE the early days of desktop publishing has been for desktop technologies to reach further and further into the publishing process. First, desktop tools replaced dedicated typesetting systems. Next, more and more line art began to be produced using desktop tools. Interfaces between desktop systems and high-end scanners were the next to appear, allowing desktop systems to use photographic imagery with the same quality attainable by high-end systems.

But these are all front-end tasks that are performed as part of making up the page. More recently, desktop technology has begun to extend its reach into back-end tasks such as trapping and imposition, as discussed in Chapters 20 and 21. Front-end systems will undoubtedly continue to improve, with more sophisticated typographic control, greater automation in database-driven applications such as catalog publishing, and continual improvements in color fidelity between monitors, desktop color printers, and the press itself, but some of the most far-reaching changes will be spurred by desktop technology's continued incursions into back-end processes.

One of the most significant developments promises to be direct-to-plate imaging, which cuts out the entire process of producing film negatives, and instead produces printing plates directly from digital files. There are some roadblocks that have as yet prevented direct-to-plate imaging from becoming commonplace, the most notable being the difficulty of producing accurate prepress proofs without film, and the lack of plate materials for digital printers that would be suitable for long print runs, but these are likely to be temporary setbacks rather than permanent barriers.

The direct-to-plate approach has several advantages. It saves money by eliminating the cost of film and processing, and, likewise, saves time by cutting out an entire stage in the production process. It should also result in a higher-quality product, since it eliminates the variables that are introduced when plates are produced optically from negatives.

Some press manufacturers have taken the direct-to-plate concept one step further by imaging the plates from digital files after they've already been mounted on the press. This direct-to-press approach is particularly useful for color printing, since it eliminates the need to make manual adjustments for plate registration. As a result, the printer can offer much shorter runs of color print jobs than would otherwise be economically feasible: Makeready is a time-consuming process for color jobs, so the print run has to be long enough to pay for the makeready. Until recently, it made little economic sense to use four-color printing for runs of less than 5,000 impressions, but now runs as short as 500 impressions can be priced competitively.

The direct-to-press approach and the continuing improvements in color laser printers combine to offer the possibility of an entirely new market in short-run color publishing, using color laser printers for very short runs and presses for slightly longer ones. Numerous studies have shown that well-designed color materials have more impact and communicate more effectively than black and white materials, a major consideration for anyone vying for the reader's attention.

The ability to produce small numbers of a piece economically also opens the door to two other strategies, distributed printing and on-demand printing. Distributed printing is already used by several major newspapers. The bulk of the newspaper is produced electronically, then sent via phone lines (or modem) or satellite to regional printing plants where material specific to the region is inserted, and the whole newspaper is printed. This allows for great savings in the cost of distribution—the finished product has less distance to travel—and also the production of regional issues of the newspaper that accommodate local advertising.

A great deal of fast-changing information is also committed to print. For example, every auto dealership has its repair manuals and parts catalogs that require frequent updating. In the past, such materials were printed in large numbers, and regular updates were sent in the form of page inserts for the binders. Stacks of paper sat around taking up space, and someone had to spend time and energy keeping track of the updates. With on-demand printing, the pieces are sent in digital form from a central location and printed as needed at the target sites using high-speed laser printers that can print both sides of the paper, collate multiple copies, and bind the finished product. The information is always up to date, and no space is wasted on large stacks of outdated documents.

Print still has a long future ahead of it, but we'd be remiss if we didn't at least touch on some of the alternative publishing media that are just beginning to appear, such as CD-ROM. At present, most CD-ROM publishing is based on reference works such as dictionaries and encyclopedias, where having the information in digital form allows much more flexibility in searching for and finding the information you want, but CD-ROM novels are beginning to appear too. One of the more intriguing aspects of CD-ROM publishing is that text is no longer confined to the linear structure of a book: Readers can find their own pathway through the story, and read the same story many times without ever reading it exactly the same way. In Chapter 23, we touch briefly on some of the exciting developments that promise to change the face of publishing.

Last, but by no means least, is an account of how we produced this book, for this is an example of desktop publishing in action. In Chapter 24, we look at both the tools and the process that went into the production of the pages you are holding in your hands.

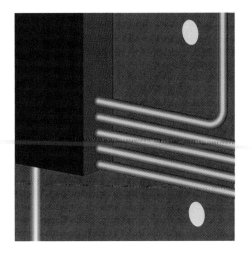

Future Directions

T'S LIKELY THAT one day in the not-too-distant future, the term *desktop publishing* will lose its meaning. There will only be *publishing*, because desktop processes will have become so ubiquitous that they will simply be the normal method of producing pages. Desktop technology is reaching ever further into the production process, and direct-to-plate imaging takes it one step further still.

Direct-to-plate imaging cuts out the time and expense of making film negatives by producing the printing plates directly from the digital data, using a device very similar to a laser printer. In a more radical implementation, direct-to-press printing, blank plates are mounted on the press, then imaged in place. This removes the need to adjust the plates on the press to ensure good registration—the plates are automatically registered—so makeready time on the press is cut dramatically, and as a result, it's possible for the printer to offer much shorter print runs at a competitive price.

Distributed publishing is already used by some major national newspapers and magazines. In addition to inserting local news sections in each regional edition, publishers can offer advertisers targeted local or regional coverage at a fraction of the cost of national ads. The national edition is produced at the main office and is then sent via modem or satellite link to the regional bureaus, where local advertising and editorial sections are inserted prior to printing.

CD-ROM publishing, while still in its infancy, promises to be an even bigger breakthrough. CD-ROM discs can hold more information than printed media; for example, one disc can hold a year's supply of a magazine. CD-ROM publications are designed to be read on a computer; the best examples are equipped with a graphical user interface and a pointing device such as a mouse. The publication might simply represent printed pages on the screen, but instead of turning one page and going on to the next, users can point to items that interest them and instantly be presented with a screenful of information. CD-ROM publications can include audio and video segments in addition to text and pictures. This may seem farfetched, and we certainly don't envisage the demise of print any time soon, but the first few CD-ROM titles have already appeared, and the possibilities for the future are boundless.

How Direct-to-Plate Imaging Works

Direct-to-Plate Imaging

1 The publication files are produced as they would be for final film output to fully imposed signatures, but instead of being sent to an imagesetter, they are sent to a digital platemaker. The platemaker works like a laser printer but uses special photosensitive plate material instead of paper and toner.

2 The platemaker produces printing plates that are ready for mounting on the press.

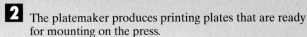
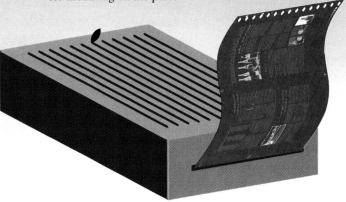

Direct-to-Press Imaging

1 In direct-to-press printing, the files are prepared for final output and are sent to the press computer, which then sends the appropriate data to the imaging head for each color.

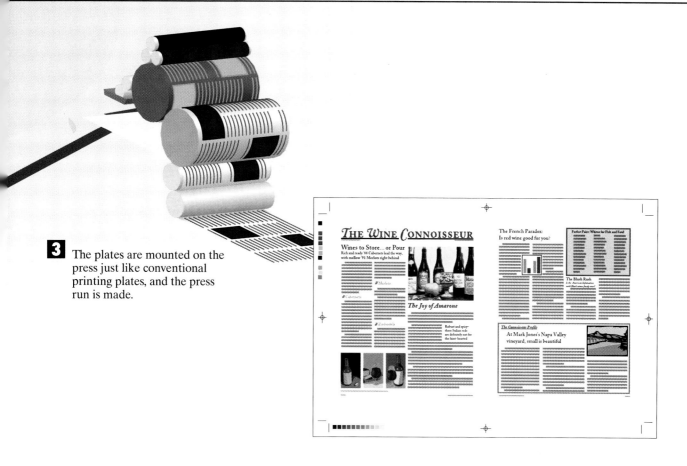

3 The plates are mounted on the press just like conventional printing plates, and the press run is made.

2 Special blank plates are mounted on the press, and then the imaging heads burn the page image onto the plate. Current approaches use a spark-discharge technology in which the image is literally burned onto the plates with minute sparks of electricity, but laser-driven technologies are under development. These should give a higher-quality result than the spark-discharge method.

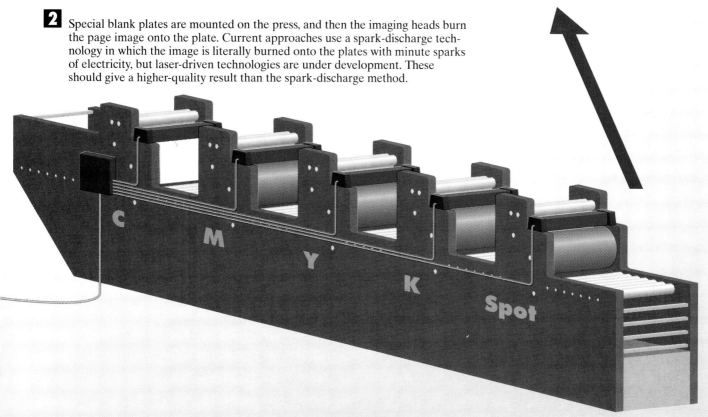

How Distributed Publishing Works

The main body of the publication is prepared electronically at the head office, and is then sent to the local offices via telephone or satellite link. Regional advertising and editorial material is prepared locally, and is inserted into each regional edition, which is printed locally. Distribution costs are reduced, and each region receives targeted local coverage.

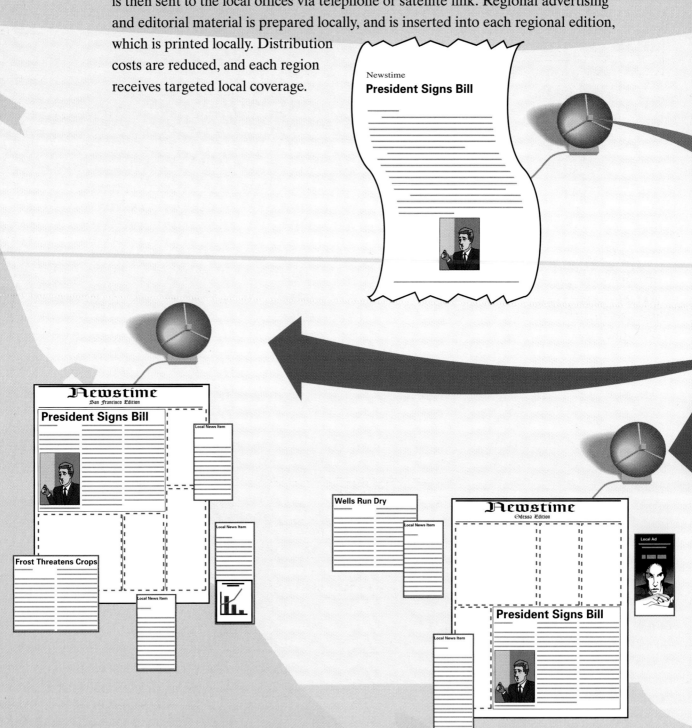

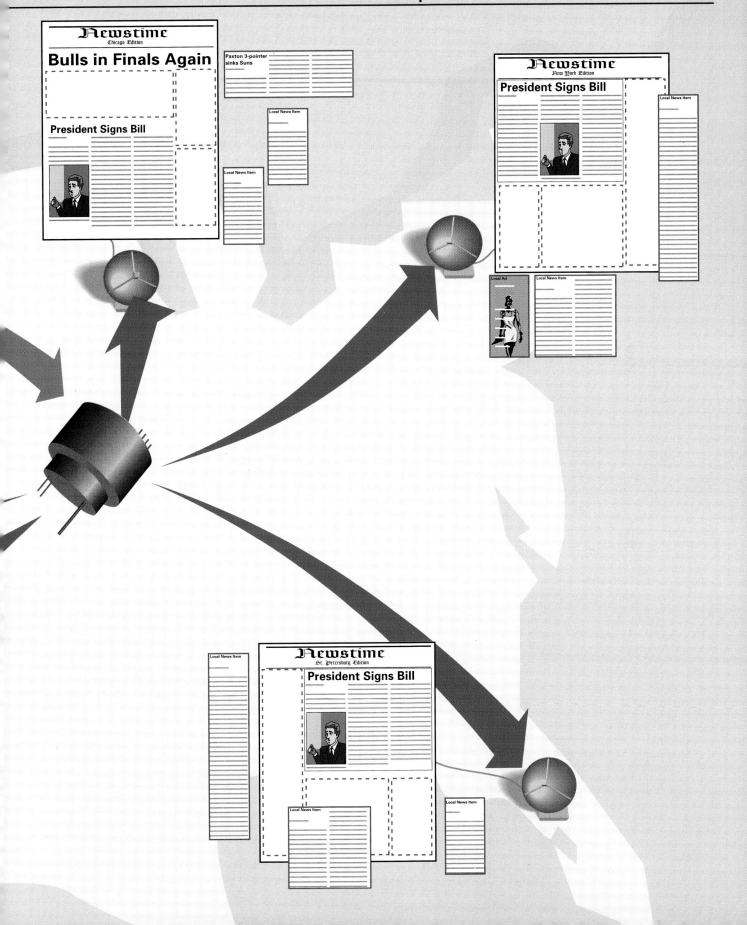

How CD-ROM Publishing Works

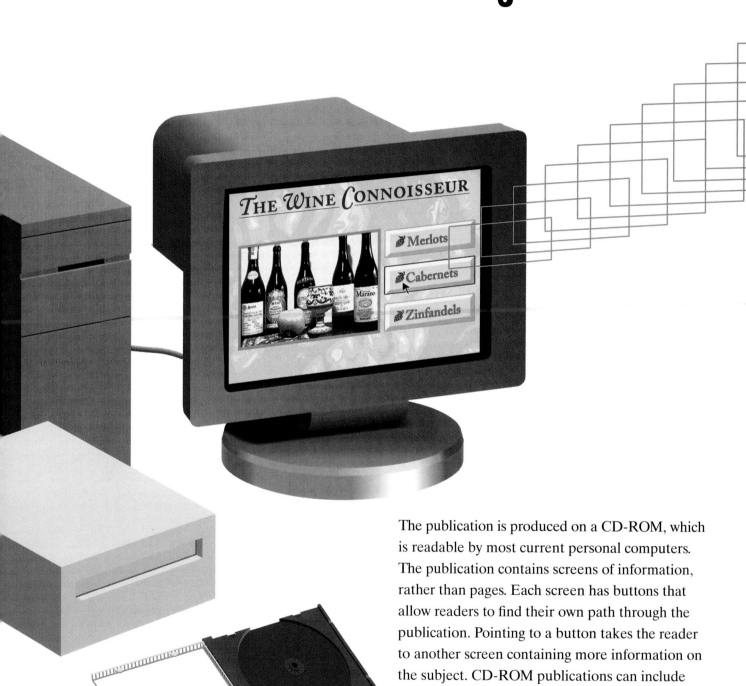

The publication is produced on a CD-ROM, which is readable by most current personal computers. The publication contains screens of information, rather than pages. Each screen has buttons that allow readers to find their own path through the publication. Pointing to a button takes the reader to another screen containing more information on the subject. CD-ROM publications can include audio and video segments in addition to text and pictures. Anything—a word, a picture, a video clip—can be a button.

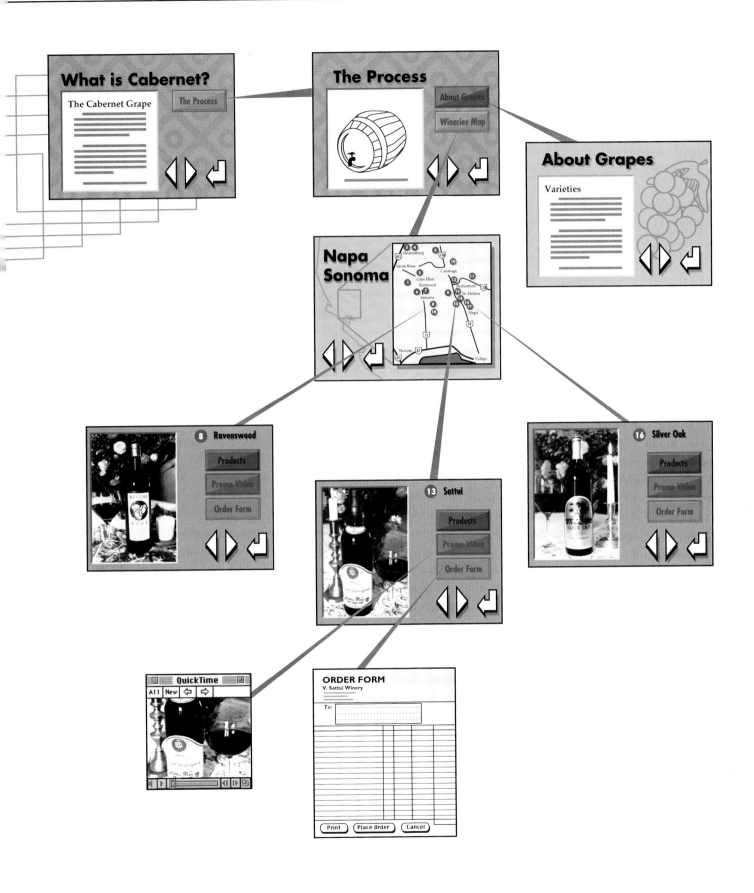

How We Produced This Book

LIKE MANY BOOKS published today, *How Desktop Publishing Works* was produced with desktop publishing tools. Text, illustrations, and layouts were all done on Macintosh computers. During the production phase, Macs linked to an imagesetter produced negative films, which were then sent to the print shop for printing on high-speed presses.

And as with many desktop-published books on the market today, traditional tools and methods also contributed to the process. Copy was submitted on paper and sent by mail to editors 20 miles away. Editorial comments were attached to hard copy with yellow sticky notes and the edited manuscript was circulated in file folders. Imposition was done by the printer in the traditional way, and, of course, the end result—this book—is still ink on paper.

Desktop publishing is more than just a collection of hardware and software cobbled together to mimic traditional systems. Networks must be fast enough to transfer large amounts of data; strategies must be devised to send and receive printed and electronic materials quickly and easily; systems must be in place to track revisions of art and text; and above all, editors, writers, and artists must cooperate.

Developing processes is perhaps the hardest aspect of establishing a desktop publishing system (for example, standardizing file-naming conventions is no small task), and despite the huge advances in hardware and software technology, managing the flow of work still remains the stumbling block of many publishing houses. As a result, each publishing house develops a system that works for its own combination of people and tools—and as desktop publishing technology evolves, so do the systems.

We can only imagine how the process of writing this book would have changed had we been allowed to send text to our editors electronically via modem, or had we been able to use teleconferencing to conduct art discussions instead of trying to coordinate meetings with people from all over the San Francisco Bay Area. We can picture printing this book according to sales demands (we hope there are a lot!) or creating targeted editions specifically for Macintosh or PC users. Eventually you may even see this book on CD-ROM or some other electronic distribution medium, with built-in animations of working presses and hypertext links walking you through the production of this book.

The future is closer than you think.

Desktop Publishing This Book

1 The authors write text on Macintosh desktop and notebook computers, then print the text on a laser printer. The hard copy, pen sketches of illustrations, and photocopied supplemental materials, along with a disk containing the text, are sent via mail or courier to the editor 20 miles away.

2 The authors also provide some original art, such as sample page layouts and digital photography. For the latter, photographic prints are scanned at 266 dpi (twice the 133-lpi screen) then retouched with image-editing software and corrected with a color-adjusted monitor. The final digital files are about 6 megabytes apiece.

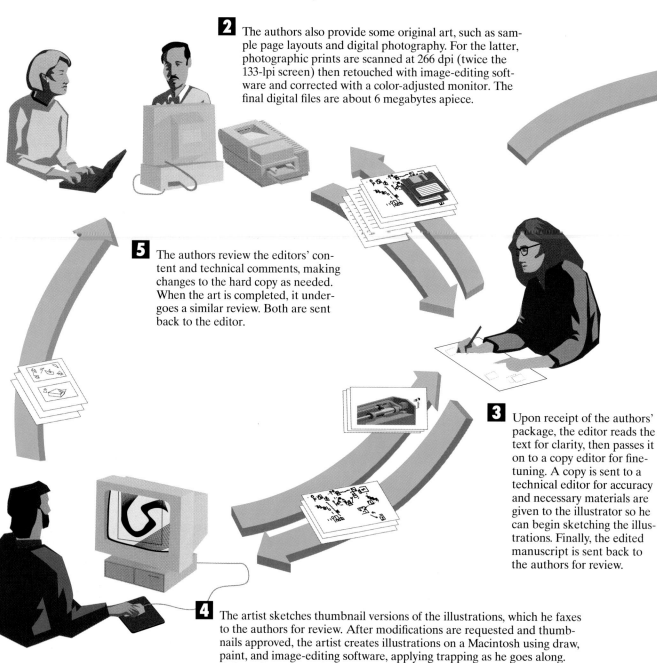

5 The authors review the editors' content and technical comments, making changes to the hard copy as needed. When the art is completed, it undergoes a similar review. Both are sent back to the editor.

3 Upon receipt of the authors' package, the editor reads the text for clarity, then passes it on to a copy editor for fine-tuning. A copy is sent to a technical editor for accuracy and necessary materials are given to the illustrator so he can begin sketching the illustrations. Finally, the edited manuscript is sent back to the authors for review.

4 The artist sketches thumbnail versions of the illustrations, which he faxes to the authors for review. After modifications are requested and thumbnails approved, the artist creates illustrations on a Macintosh using draw, paint, and image-editing software, applying trapping as he goes along. Color printouts are given back to the editor for comments before they're mailed back to the authors.

6 The editor reviews all comments and then gives the edited copy along with the original disk to the word processor, who enters changes and formats the text for layout. The artist makes requested changes to the illustration.

7 Disks containing the corrected, formatted text and final illustrations now go to the production department. The layout artist places text and graphics in a page layout program and then designs the pages, using templates and artistic vision to determine the look of the page. The integrated pages are printed out, then mailed to the authors for final approval and sign-off.

8 After final corrections and polishing, the pages are output on a high-resolution (2400 dpi) imagesetter, which produces negative films at a 133-line screen. Integral laminated proofs are made at a service bureau, then the film is sent to a press for printing.

9 *How Desktop Publishing Works* is printed using four colors on a web-feed press; the pages are then folded, cut, and gathered into 16-page signatures. Finally, it's perfect bound.

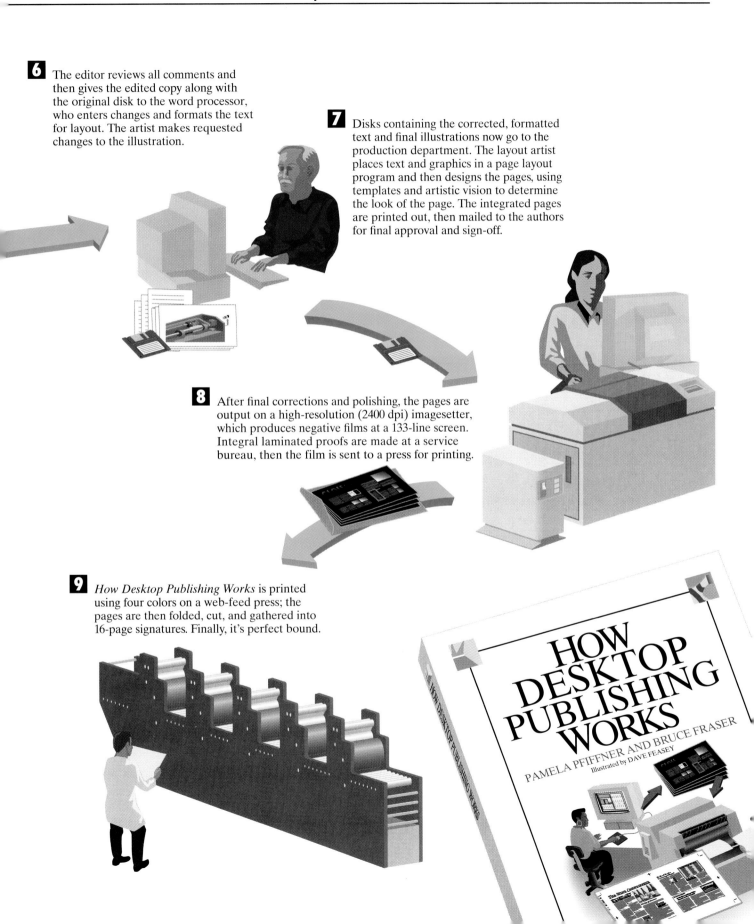

HOW DESKTOP PUBLISHING WORKS

PAMELA PFIFFNER AND BRUCE FRASER
Illustrated by DAVE FEASEY

Folios in italics refer to illustrated pages

A

absolute positioning devices, *123*

additive primary colors, 87, *90*

Adobe Mythos type style, *39*

Adobe Type Manager (ATM), 44

alignment

    page, *53*

    registration, 147, 159, *160–161*, 177

alphabets, 5, *8*

analog-to-digital converters

    in digital cameras, *124*

    in scanners, 113, *116–117*

anchor points, *79*

area arrays, *124*

arrays, CCD

    in digital cameras, *124*

    in scanners, 113–114, *116–117*

artistic designers, 26

artists, 11, *14, 16*

ascenders, *38*

ASCII character set, 44, *48*

audio in CD-ROM publishing, 177

automatic page numbering, *52*

B

backgrounds for color, *91*

backups, drives for, 129, *130–131*

banners, *32*

baselines, *38*

Baskerville, John, 6

Bernoulli drives, 129, *131*

Bezier curves, *47*

bindery process, *151*

bit depth, 69

bitmap fonts, 43–44, *46*

bitmaps vs. raster images, 69, *70*

bits (binary digits), 43, *70*

blanket cylinders, 149, *150*

Bodoni, Giambattista, 6

Bodoni type style, *39*

body type, *32*, 35, *53*

Bookman type style, *39*

bottling, 163, *165*

bowls, *39*

boxes, *33*

Brainerd, Paul, 2, 11

brightness, 88, *92*

C

camera operators, *15*

cameras, digital, 109, 121, *124–125*

caps, *32*, 36, *38, 49*

capstan imagesetters, *140*

captions, *33*

cartridges, printer, *136*

Caslon, William, 6

CCD (charge-coupled devices)

    in digital cameras, *124*

    in scanners, 113–114, *116–117*

CD-ROM
    future of, 175, 177, *182–183*
    Photo CD, 109, 121, *126–127*
    for software distribution, 129, *130*
character formats, 51, *53*
character sets, 44, *48–49*
chokes, 159, *161*
CIE color spaces, 102
clipping paths, *79*
CMYK colors, 95
    operation of, *98–99*
    from RGB, 101, *104–105*
cold type, 7
color, 58–59, 63, 84–85
    additive and subtractive, *90*
    complementary, *93*
    computer, 101–102, *104–105*
    context of, *91*
    models, 87–88
    printed, 6–7, 95, *150. See also* color printers
    process, 59, *66*, 95, *98–99*
    spot colors, 59, *66*, 95, *96–97*
    trapping for, 159, *160–161*
color gamuts, *104*
color images, *71*, 129
color-management systems, *105*
color-matching engines, *105*
color monitors, 101, *104–105*

color printers, *23*, 133–134
    dye-sublimation, *142–143*
    ink-jet, *136*
    for proofing, 168
    thermal-wax, *142*
color scanning, 113, *116, 119*
color screens, *156–157*
color separations, 64, *66*, 146–147, 153, *154–157*
color spaces, *92*
color wheel, *93*
column guides, *52*
complementary colors, *93*
composing sticks, 6
composite proofs, 167, *171*
comps, *23*, 133
computer-aided design (CAD), 121
computers, *22*
    color on, 101–102, *104–105*
    graphics on, 69, *70–73*
context of color, *91*
continuous-roll paper, 6, *9*
continuous-tone images, 59, 63, *66*
contract proofs, 147
control points, *79*
costs, 29
counter, *39*
counterpunches, *38*
cutting in bindery process, *151*
cylinders, 149, *150*

D

data compression, *131*

decks, *32*

descenders, *38*

design, 26

designers, 11, *14, 16*

developer rollers, *138–139*

device profiles, *105*

digital audio tape (DAT), 129, *131*

digital cameras, 109, 121, *124–125*

digital platemakers, *178*

digital printers, *154–155*

digital proofing, 167, *170*

digital type and fonts, *9*, 26–27, 43–45, *46–49*

dingbats fonts, *48*

direct digital color proofing (DDCP), 167, *170*

direct-to-plate imaging, 174, 177, *178–179*

direct-to-press approach, 174–175, 177, *178–179*

display type, *33*, 35, *39*

distributed publishing, 175, 177, *180–181*

dithering, *98*

dot-matrix printers, 110

drives for backups, 129, *130–131*

drum imagesetters, *141*

drum scanners, *22*, 109, 113–114, *118–119*

drums in laser printers, *138–139*

dummies, 26

duotones, *97*

dye-sublimation printers

operation of, 134, *142–143*

for proofing, 168

E

editors, 11, *14*

electronic prepress shops, 146

expert character sets, *49*

extended character set, 44, *48*

extruding graphics, *80*

eyebrows, *33*

F

facing pages, *52*

figures, old-style, *49*

film, *17*

film processors, *141*

film strippers, 58

first line indents, *53*

flatbed scanners, *22*, 109, 113, *116*

flush left/ragged right justification, 36

folios, *32*

fonts, 20, *22*, 43–44, *46–49, 53*, 129. *See also* typefaces

free-form drawings, 121

freehand tool, *79*

fuser rollers

in dye-sublimation printers, *143*

in laser printers, *138–139*

in thermal-wax printers, *142*

Futura type style, *39*

future directions, 174–175, 177

   CD-ROM publishing, *182–183*

   direct-to-plate imaging, *178–179*

   distributed publishing, *180–181*

G

galleys, 11, *14*

Garamond, Claude, 6

Garamond type style, *39*

glyphs, 45, *49*

graphic input devices, 121

   digital cameras, *124–125*

   Photo CD systems, *126–127*

   tablets, *122–123*

graphics, 51, 58–60

   computer, 69, *70–73*

   in page layout programs, *54–55*

   resolution, *55, 81*

   traditional, 63–64, *66–67*

graphics programs, *22*, 75

   illustration, *78–79*

   image-editing, *77*

   paint, *76*

   three-dimensional, *80–81*

graphics tablets, 109, 121, *122–123*

gravure, 149, *151*

gray-scale images, 69, *70*

grids, 29, *32–33*

guides, column, *52*

Gutenberg, Johannes, 5

gutters, *33*

H

halftones, 6–7, *9*

   in color, 95, *97–98*, 153, *154–155*

   in gravure, *151*

   interference patterns with, *156–157*

   in prepress process, 146–147

hand-held scanners, 109

hard disks, *22*, 129

hardware, 108–110

   graphic input devices, 121, *122–127*

   printers, 133–134, *136–143*

   scanners, 113–114, *116–119*

   storage devices, 129, *130–131*

heading style, *53*

headline type, *33*, 35

heating elements in ink-jet printers, *137*

high resolution graphics, *55, 81*

hot type, 6

How Desktop Publishing Works, production of, 185, *186–187*

hue, 88, *92*

hyphenation, *41*

hyphenation zones, 36

I

illuminated manuscripts, 5, *8*

illustration programs, 75, *78–79*

image-editing programs, 75, *77*

imagesetters, 12, *23*, 110, 134

    halftone dots with, *154*

    operation of, *140–141*

ImageWriter I printer, 11

imposition, 147, 163, *164–165*

impression cylinders, 149, *150*

indents, *53*

infographics, 58

initial caps, *32*

ink colors, *150*

ink-jet printers, 19, *22*, 133

    operation of, *136–137*

    for proofing, 168

input devices, 19, 108–109, 121

    digital cameras, *124–125*

    Photo CD systems, *126–127*

    scanners, 113–114, *116–119*

    tablets, *122–123*

instances, font, *47*

intaglio printing, 149

integral proofs, 167, *171*

interference patterns, 153, *156–157*

italics style, 6

J

justified text, 36

K

kerning, *41*

keyboards, 19

knife tool, *79*

knockouts, 159, *161*

laser printers, 19, *22*, 110, 133, *138–139*

LaserWriter printer, 11–12

lathing, *80*

layout. *See* page layout; page layout programs

leading, 35, *40*, *53*

left indents, *53*

Leibling, A. J., 12

letter spacing, 36, *40*

ligatures, *47*, *49*

line art, 59, 63, *66*

line-casting machines, 6

lines in illustration programs, *79*

lines per inch (lpi), 153, *154*

linking graphics, *54–55*

Linotype machines, 6, *9*, 27

list style, *53*

lithographs, 63

local formatting, *53*

lowercase, 6

low resolution graphics, *55*, *81*

M

Macintosh computers, 19

magneto-optical drives, 129, *130*

makeready process, 149, 174

margins, *32–33*

master pages, 51, *52*

matrices, *9, 38*

measurement units, 30

mechanicals, 63, *66*

Memphis type style, *39*

metal type, 35, *38*

modelling module in 3D graphics, 75, *80*

modern type style, *39*

moire patterns, 153, *156–157*

monitor screens, 19, *22*, 101

   in color-management systems, *104–105*

   in proofing, 168, *170*

mouse, 19

movable type, 5–6, *8*

Multiple Master fonts, 45, *47*

multisession recording, *127*

N

nameplates, *32*

nested signatures, 163

newspapers

   beginning of, 6

   photographs for, *125*

Newton, Isaac, 87

nozzles in ink-jet printers, *137*

numbering pages, *52*

O

offset lithography, 149, *150*

old-style figures, *49*

old type style, *39*

on-demand printing, 175

OPC (organo-photoconductors), *139*

ornament fonts, *48*

outline fonts, 43–44, *46*

output devices

   monitors, 19, *22*, 101, *104–105*, 168, *170*

   printers. *See* printers

overlay proofs, 167, *171*

overprinting, 159, *161*

P

page-description language, 11–12, 27, 60, 75

page layout, 29–30, *32–33*

   digital fonts in, 43–45, *46–49*

   typefaces in, 35–36, *38–41*

page layout programs, 19, *22*, 26–27, 51

   disk space for, 129

   graphics in, *54–55*

   setting up documents in, *52–53*

PageMaker software, 11–12

page numbering, *52*

paint programs, 75, *76*

Pantone inks, 95

paper

   and color, 101

   continuous-roll, 6, *9*

invention of, 5

size of, 26

paperless office, 2

paragraph formats, 51, *53*

paragraph spacing, *53*

paste-up artists, *15*, 26

paths in illustration programs, 75, *78–79*

pen tool, *79*

perfect bindings, *151*, 163

perfecting presses, *15*

phosphors, 101

Photo CD Managers, *126*

Photo CD players, *127*

Photo CD scanners, *126*

Photo CD systems, 109, 121, *126–127*

Photo CD Writer, *127*

photographic process, 63

photography and photographs, 6, 121, *126–127*

phototype, 43

phototypesetting, 7, *9*

picas, 30

pixels (picture elements), 43, *76*

plate cylinders, *150*

platemakers, *178*

plates, 11, *15*, 58, *150*

PMT (photomultiplier tubes), 114, *118–119*

point size, 30, *53*

PostScript data files, *73*

PostScript fonts and typefaces, 27, 43–45, *47*

PostScript illustration programs, *22*, *72*, 75, *78–79*

PostScript imagesetters, 12

PostScript laser printers, *22*, 133

PostScript page-description language, 11–12, 27, 60, 75

prepress, *23*, 146–147

color separations, 153, *154–157*

imposition, 163, *164–165*

proofing, 167–168, *170–171*

trapping, 159, *160–161*

press operators, *15*, *17*

press proofs, 167, *171*

pressure-sensitive styli, *123*

previews in graphics, *81*

primary colors, 87, *90–91*

primitives, *80*

printed color, 6–7, 95, *150*. *See also* printers

Printer Control Language (PCL), 60

printers, 19, *22–23*, 108–110, 133–134

digital, *154–155*

dye-sublimation, *142–143*

fonts in, 43–44

halftone dots with, *154–155*

imagesetters, *140–141*

ink-jet, *136–137*

laser, *138–139*

for proofing, 168

thermal-wax, *142*

print heads

in dye-sublimation printers, *143*

in ink-jet printers, *136*

in thermal-wax printers, *142*

printing presses, 5–6, *8–9*, 58, 149, *150–151*.
　　See also prepress
process color, 59, *66*, 95
　　operation of, *98–99*
　　trapping, *160*, *161*
production artists, 26
proofing, *17*, 133, 147, 167–168, *170–171*
publishing history, 2–3, 5–7
pucks, 121, *122*
pull quotes, *33*
punches, *38*

Q

quadratic splines, *47*
QuickDraw program, 60
quotes, *49*

R

ragged right justification, 36
raster graphics, 59, 75, *76*
raster image processors, *23*, *140*
raster images, 69, *70–71*
rasterizers, 43–44, *47*
reference color space, *105*
reflective colors, 87
registration, 147, 159
　　with direct-to-press printing, 177
　　operation of, *160–161*
removable media, 109, 129, *130–131*
rendering module in 3D graphics, 75, *80–81*

resolution and halftone dots, *155*
resolution-independent graphics, 60
RGB color model, 101, *104–105*
ribbons
　　in dye-sublimation printers, *143*
　　in thermal-wax printers, *142*
right indents, *53*
RIP (raster image processors), *23*, *140*
roman style, 6
rotary presses, *9*
rotogravure, 149
rules, *33*
running heads, *32*, *52*

S

saddle-stitched bindings, *151*, 163
sans serif fonts, 35–36, *39*
saturation, 88, *92*
scalable fonts, *46*
scanners, 19–20, *22*, 108–109, 113–114
　　drum, *118–119*
　　flatbed, *116*
　　Photo CD, *126*
　　resolution of, *155*
　　transparency, *117*
scanning, color, 113, *116*, *119*
scanning heads, 113, *116*, *118*
screen angle, 153, *156–157*
screen frequency, *98*, 153, *154*
screens, color, 156–157

separations, color, 64, *66*, 146–147, 153, *154–157*

sequential-access media, *131*

serif fonts, 35, *38–39*

service bureaus, 12, *17*

shapes in illustration programs, 75, *78–79*

shingling, 163, *165*

shoulders, *38*

signatures, *15*, 147, *151*, 163, *164–165*

size

   of paper, 26

   of type, 12, 30, 36, *53*

slab serif type style, *39*

slide scanners, *22*, 109, 113–114, *117*

slugs, 6, *9*, *38*

small caps, *49*

soft proofing, 168, *170*

software, 19, *22*. *See also* graphics programs;
   page layout programs

spacing, 36, *40*, *53*

spot colors, 59, *66*, 95

   operation of, *96–97*

   printing, 133

   trapping with, 159, *161*

spreads, *32*, 159, *161*

stacked signatures, 163

stepper motors, 113, *116*

storage devices, *22*, 108–109, 129, *130–131*

strippers, film, 58

styles, *53*

style sheets, 51

styli, 121, *122–123*

subheads, *32*

subtractive primary colors, 87, *90*

surface maps, *81*

swashes, *49*

SyQuest drives, 129, *131*

T

tablets, 109, 121, *122–123*

tabs, *53*

templates, *16*

text wrap, *54*

thermal-wax printers, 134, *142*

three-dimensional graphics programs, 75, *80–81*

tints, *97*

toner, *138–139*

tracking, *41*

transitional type style, *39*

transmissive colors, 87

transparency scanners, *22*, 109, 113–114, *117*

trapping, 147, 159, *160–161*

TrueType fonts, 27, 43–45, *47*

TrueType GX format, 45, *47*

typefaces, 6, 20, *22*, 26–27, 35–36, *38–39*. *See also* fonts

typesetters, 11, *14*

typesetting, 6

type size, 12, 30, 36, *53*

type styles, *39*

typographer's quotes, *49*

typography, 26, 35

U

Unicode character set, 44

uppercase, 6

V

vector graphics, 59, 69, *72–73*

video in CD-ROM publishing, 177, *183*

W

web, *6*

web presses, *9, 151*

white light, *90*

Windows operating system, 19

wire frames, 75, *80–81*

word processing programs, *22,* 51

word spacing, 36, *40, 53*

writers, 11, *14, 16*

writing, 5

WYSIWYG (what-you-see-is-what-you-get)
    operating systems, 19, 84

X

X-height, *38*

The Quick and Easy Way to Learn.

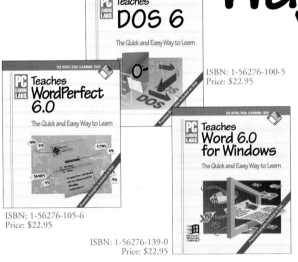

ISBN: 1-56276-100-5
Price: $22.95

ISBN: 1-56276-105-6
Price: $22.95

ISBN: 1-56276-139-0
Price: $22.95

We know that PC Learning Labs books are the fastest and easiest way to learn because years have been spent perfecting them. Beginners will find practice sessions that are easy to follow and reference information that is easy to find. Even the most computer-shy readers can gain confidence faster than they ever thought possible.

The time we spent designing this series translates into time saved for you. You can feel confident that the information is accurate and presented in a way that allows you to learn quickly and effectively.

ISBN: 1-56276-122-6
Price: $22.95

ISBN: 1-56276-176-5
Price: $22.95

ISBN: 1-56276-148-X
Price: $22.95

ISBN: 1-56276-135-8
Price: $22.95

ISBN: 1-56276-020-3
Price: $22.95

ISBN: 1-56276-134-X
Price: $22.95

ISBN: 1-56276-124-2
Price: $22.95

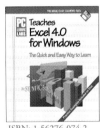

ISBN: 1-56276-074-2
Price: $22.95

ISBN: 1-56276-033-5
Price: $22.95

ISBN: 1-56276-051-3
Price: $22.95

ISBN: 1-56276-154-4
Price: $22.95

ISBN: 1-56276-138-2
Price: $22.95

Also available: Titles featuring new versions of Excel, 1-2-3, Access, Microsoft Project, Ami Pro, and new applications, pending software release. Call 1-800-688-0448 for title update information.

Available at all fine bookstores, or by calling 1-800-688-0448, ext. 103.

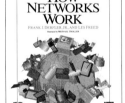

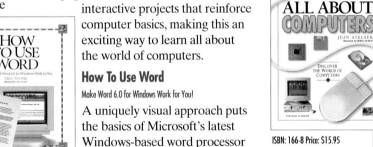

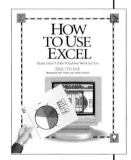

ATTENTION TEACHERS AND TRAINERS
Now You Can Teach From These Books!

ZD Press now offers instructors and trainers
the materials they need to use these books in their classes.

- An Instructor's Manual features flexible lessons designed for use in a 10- or 15-week course (30-45 course hours).

- Student exercises and tests on floppy disk provide you with an easy way to tailor and/or duplicate tests as you need them.

- A Transparency Package contains all the graphics from the book, each on a single, full-color transparency.

- Spanish edition of *PC/Computing How Computers Work* will be available.

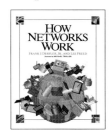
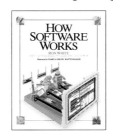
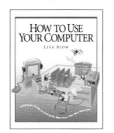
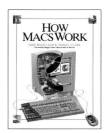

Ziff-Davis Press Survey of Readers

Please help us in our effort to produce the best books on personal computing.
For your assistance, we would be pleased to send you a FREE catalog
featuring the complete line of Ziff-Davis Press books.

1. How did you first learn about this book?

Recommended by a friend . . . . ☐ -1 (5)

Recommended by store personnel . . . . ☐ -2

Saw in Ziff-Davis Press catalog . . . . ☐ -3

Received advertisement in the mail . . . . ☐ -4

Saw the book on bookshelf at store . . . . ☐ -5

Read book review in: _____ ☐ -6

Saw an advertisement in: _____ ☐ -7

Other (Please specify): _____ ☐ -8

2. Which THREE of the following factors most influenced your decision to purchase this book? (Please check up to THREE.)

Front or back cover information on book . . . ☐ -1 (6)

Logo of magazine affiliated with book . . . . . . ☐ -2

Special approach to the content . . . . ☐ -3

Completeness of content . . . . ☐ -4

Author's reputation. ☐ -5

Publisher's reputation . . . . ☐ -6

Book cover design or layout . . . . ☐ -7

Index or table of contents of book . . . . ☐ -8

Price of book . . . . ☐ -9

Special effects, graphics, illustrations . . . . ☐ -0

Other (Please specify): _____ ☐ -x

3. How many computer books have you purchased in the last six months? _____ (7-10)

4. On a scale of 1 to 5, where 5 is excellent, 4 is above average, 3 is average, 2 is below average, and 1 is poor, please rate each of the following aspects of this book below. (Please circle your answer.)

Depth/completeness of coverage   5 4 3 2 1   (11)

Organization of material   5 4 3 2 1   (12)

Ease of finding topic   5 4 3 2 1   (13)

Special features/time saving tips   5 4 3 2 1   (14)

Appropriate level of writing   5 4 3 2 1   (15)

Usefulness of table of contents   5 4 3 2 1   (16)

Usefulness of index   5 4 3 2 1   (17)

Usefulness of accompanying disk   5 4 3 2 1   (18)

Usefulness of illustrations/graphics 5 4 3 2 1 (19)

Cover design and attractiveness   5 4 3 2 1   (20)

Overall design and layout of book   5 4 3 2 1   (21)

Overall satisfaction with book   5 4 3 2 1   (22)

5. Which of the following computer publications do you read regularly; that is, 3 out of 4 issues?

Byte . . . . ☐ -1 (23)

Computer Shopper . . . . ☐ -2

Corporate Computing . . . . ☐ -3

Dr. Dobb's Journal . . . . ☐ -4

LAN Magazine . . . . ☐ -5

MacWEEK . . . . ☐ -6

MacUser . . . . ☐ -7

PC Computing . . . . ☐ -8

PC Magazine . . . . ☐ -9

PC WEEK . . . . ☐ -0

Windows Sources . . . . ☐ -x

Other (Please specify): _____ ☐ -y

Please turn page.

6. What is your level of experience with personal computers? With the subject of this book?

	With PCs	With subject of book
Beginner	☐ -1 (24)	☐ -1 (25)
Intermediate	☐ -2	☐ -2
Advanced	☐ -3	☐ -3

7. Which of the following best describes your job title?

Officer (CEO/President/VP/owner) ☐ -1 (26)
Director/head ☐ -2
Manager/supervisor ☐ -3
Administration/staff ☐ -4
Teacher/educator/trainer ☐ -5
Lawyer/doctor/medical professional ☐ -6
Engineer/technician ☐ -7
Consultant ☐ -8
Not employed/student/retired ☐ -9
Other (Please specify): _____ ☐ -0

8. What is your age?

Under 20 ☐ -1 (27)
21-29 ☐ -2
30-39 ☐ -3
40-49 ☐ -4
50-59 ☐ -5
60 or over ☐ -6

9. Are you:

Male ☐ -1 (28)
Female ☐ -2

Thank you for your assistance with this important information! Please write your address below to receive our free catalog.

Name: _____
Address: _____
City/State/Zip: _____

Fold here to mail.

1919-03-08

_____
_____
_____

BUSINESS REPLY MAIL
FIRST CLASS MAIL   PERMIT NO. 1612   OAKLAND, CA

POSTAGE WILL BE PAID BY ADDRESSEE

Ziff-Davis Press

5903 Christie Avenue
Emeryville, CA 94608-1925
Attn: Marketing

NO POSTAGE
NECESSARY
IF MAILED IN
THE UNITED
STATES

Cut Here

Cut He